EXECUTIVE SUMMARY

The Socialist Republic of Vietnam is an authoritarian state ruled by a single party, the Communist Party of Vietnam (CPV), and led by General Secretary Nguyen Phu Trong, Prime Minister Nguyen Xuan Phuc, President Tran Dai Quang, and Chairwoman of the National Assembly Nguyen Thi Kim Ngan. The most recent National Assembly elections, held on May 22, were neither free nor fair, despite limited competition among CPV-vetted candidates.

Civilian authorities maintained effective control over the security forces.

The National Assembly delayed the implementation of several laws passed in 2015 affecting the rights of citizens, including a new penal code, criminal procedure code, and law on custody and temporary detention.

The most significant human rights problems in the country were severe government restrictions of citizens' political rights, particularly their right to change their government through free and fair elections; limits on citizens' civil liberties, including freedom of assembly, association, and expression; and inadequate protection of citizens' due process rights, including protection against arbitrary detention.

Other human rights abuses included arbitrary and unlawful deprivation of life; police attacks and corporal punishment; arbitrary arrest and detention for political activities; continued police mistreatment of suspects during arrest and detention, including the use of lethal force and austere prison conditions; and denial of the right to a fair and expeditious trial. The judicial system was opaque and lacked independence, and political and economic influences regularly affected judicial outcomes. The government limited freedom of speech and suppressed dissent; exercised control over and censored the press; restricted internet freedom and freedom of religion; maintained often-heavy surveillance of activists; and continued to limit privacy rights and freedoms of assembly, association, and movement. The government continued to control registration of nongovernmental organizations (NGOs) closely, including human rights organizations. Authorities restricted visits by human rights NGOs and foreign press agencies that did not agree to government oversight. Corruption remained widespread throughout public-sector institutions, including police. The government maintained limits on workers' rights to form and join independent unions and did not enforce safe and healthy working conditions adequately. Child labor persisted, especially in agricultural occupations.

The government sometimes took corrective action, including prosecutions, against officials who violated the law, and police officers sometimes acted with impunity.

Section 1. Respect for the Integrity of the Person, Including Freedom from:

a. Arbitrary Deprivation of Life and Other Unlawful or Politically Motivated Killings

There were multiple reports indicating officials or other agents under the command of the Ministry of Public Security or provincial public security departments committed arbitrary or unlawful killings, including reports of at least nine deaths of persons in custody. In most cases authorities either provided little information regarding investigations into these deaths or stated the deaths were the result of suicide or medical problems. In a small number of cases, the government held police officials responsible. Despite guidance from the Supreme People's Court to charge police officers responsible for causing deaths in custody with murder, such officers typically faced lesser charges.

On March 25, Y Sik Nie died at Cu M'gar district hospital, Dak Lak Province, after more than three months of detention by local police. In December 2015 authorities took Nie to a local police station for theft allegations; his family was not able to visit him until March 25, when a family friend informed them that Nie was in critical condition at a local hospital. When the family arrived at the hospital, they found him dead. The family told media that Nie was a very healthy man before his arrest and that an autopsy indicated injury to his internal organs. Police and hospital staff denied the family access to his medical records. On May 27, Dak Lak provincial authorities announced Nie died of heart failure; Nie's family disagreed and requested a government investigation into the death.

On July 3, Pham Quang Thien reportedly hanged himself in a detention facility in Thong Nhat district, Dong Nai Province. Authorities took Thien into custody on June 29 for allegedly stealing a tablet computer. Per media reporting, Dong Nai provincial police conducted an autopsy with a representative of Thien's family present. The examiner concluded Thien died of hanging, but Thien's family stated they had evidence Thien died from physical assault.

During the year in a small number of cases, the government held security officers responsible for arbitrary deprivation of life. On May 17, the People's Court of Dong Thap Province convicted Huynh Ngoc Tong, the former vice chief of the Police Investigation Agency of Cao Lanh City, and investigator Pham Xuan Binh of "using corporal punishment" against Nguyen Tuan Thanh. Thanh had died of his injuries sustained while in detention in 2012. The court sentenced Tong to 18 months in prison and Binh to time served in pretrial detention (11 months and 11 days). Both Tong and Binh claimed authorities forced them to confess to the charges.

Do Dang Du's lawyer and human rights organizations criticized the People's Court of Hanoi's decision to sentence Du's cellmate Vu Van Binh to 10 years in prison for "deliberately inflicting injuries" and causing Du's death, stating authorities had made Binh a scapegoat. After Du's death authorities reportedly forced the family to bury his body immediately, and the family alleged Du's autopsy report failed to include the full extent of his injuries. In October 2015, 17-year-old Do Dang Du reportedly died due to torture while in police custody in Hanoi for allegations of theft.

b. Disappearance

There were no reports of politically motivated disappearances.

c. Torture and Other Cruel, Inhuman, or Degrading Treatment or Punishment

The law prohibits physical abuse of detainees, but suspects commonly reported mistreatment and torture by police, plainclothes security officials, and drug-detention center personnel during arrest, interrogation, and detention. Police, prosecutors, and government oversight agencies seldom conducted investigations of specific reports of mistreatment.

In June 2015 the National Assembly released a report describing multiple cases of forced confessions or use of corporal punishment during police investigations from 2011 to 2014. The Ministry of Public Security reported it received 46 complaints of forced confession or use of corporal punishment; of these, authorities substantiated only three, and six remained under investigation.

In November the National Assembly delayed the implementation of the criminal procedure code, passed in November 2015, pending further revisions to the penal code.

Political and religious activists and their families alleged numerous and sometimes severe instances of harassment by Ministry of Public Security officials and agents, ranging from intimidation and insults to more significant abuses, such as physical assault during interrogation or attacks on their homes with rocks by plainclothes police. Activists also reported assaults on them and their families that caused injury and trauma requiring hospitalization. During the year there was at least one credible report that ministry officials and police in a province in the central region of the country physically beat a detained human rights activist and threatened to reveal his sexual orientation to his family members unless he ceased his advocacy activities.

On multiple occasions in January and February, plainclothes police officers in Lam Dong Province reportedly attacked human rights activist and former prisoner of conscience Tran Minh Nhat and his family members with stones, causing head injuries. From January to April, local police reportedly also verbally threatened his family members, prevented him from travelling to receive medical treatment, burned his crops, killed his livestock, and sprayed his house with pesticides.

During the year local police in Pleiku city, Gia Lai Province, reportedly harassed, assaulted, and threatened repeatedly Tran Thi Hong, the wife of imprisoned pastor Nguyen Cong Chinh. On March 30, police temporarily detained Hong and her son and locked them out of their house while they were on their way to meet foreign diplomats. From March to May, Hong reported that Pleiku city police officers assaulted her on three different occasions. On May 27 and 28, police reportedly broke into her home and forced her to attend interrogation sessions at a local police station. Local police also reportedly summoned Hong for questioning every day from June 1 through June 10. Harassment by police, including regular home searches and seizures of her personal property such as her cell phone, continued through July and August.

From April to July, police officers and plainclothes security forces in multiple locations around the country reportedly assaulted individuals attending demonstrations related to an environmental disaster that caused mass fish deaths along the central coastline. These demonstrations coincided with the period preceding National Assembly elections and the visit to the country by a foreign leader. On May 1 and May 8, police in Ho Chi Minh City reportedly detained and assaulted dozens of activists attending or attempting to join environmental demonstrations. On May 8, plainclothes police officers in Hanoi reportedly beat Ha Anh Tu, a person with disabilities, while he was participating in an environmental demonstration. On May 19, Ho Chi Minh City police reportedly assaulted activists Tran Hoang Han, Nguyen Huu Tinh, and Nguyen Phuong. On June 5-6, Ho Chi Minh City authorities reportedly detained, assaulted, and subsequently strip-searched human rights activist Tran Thu Nguyet for taking part in an environmental demonstration. On July 18, police in Phu Xuan Commune, Nha Be District, Ho Chi Minh City, reportedly detained and repeatedly assaulted activist Nguyen Phuong after Phuong participated in environmental demonstrations in May and June (see also section 1.d.).

On July 9, plainclothes security officials reportedly abducted former prisoner of conscience Nguyen Viet Dung at a hotel in Ho Chi Minh City, took him to Tan Son Nhat Airport, and forced him to buy a ticket and return to his hometown of Vinh in Nghe An Province. Upon arriving in Vinh, plainclothes police from Nghe An Province confined him in a vehicle for approximately one hour, beating him, threatening to kill him, and questioning him about his activities in Ho Chi Minh City. Dung reportedly had visited Ho Chi Minh City to protest the local government's plans to demolish the United Buddhist Church of Vietnam's Lien Tri Pagoda.

There were also numerous reports of police mistreatment and assaults against individuals who were not activists or involved in politics. For example, on March 2, plainclothes police in Hung Yen Province summoned Nguyen Van Manh to police headquarters. Police reportedly questioned Manh about an allegation of theft and subsequently assaulted him, including striking his genitalia with a police baton and crushing his fingers.

On April 4, Ho Chi Minh City police beat fruit vendor Pham Thien Minh Phong to the point of unconsciousness, resulting in brain injury and Phong's hospitalization. The leadership of the local police unit issued an apology, suspended one of the officers who beat Phong, and stated police would open an investigation into the incident.

Prison and Detention Center Conditions

Prison conditions were austere but generally not life threatening. Insufficient diet and unclean food, overcrowding, lack of access to potable water, and poor sanitation remained serious problems. According to Amnesty International and former prisoners of conscience, prison authorities singled out political prisoners, particularly in the Central Highlands and sensitive ethnic minority areas, for physical abuse, solitary confinement, denial of medical treatment, and punitive prison transfers.

Physical Conditions: Authorities generally held men and women separately, with some reported exceptions in local detention centers where space was often limited. Authorities also typically utilized separate facilities for holding pretrial detainees and convicted prisoners. Although authorities generally held juveniles in prison separately from adults, on rare occasions juveniles reportedly were held in detention with adults for short periods due to lack of space.

Prisoners had access to basic health care, although in many cases officials prevented family members from providing medication to prisoners. Family members of imprisoned activists who experienced health problems claimed medical treatment was inadequate and resulted in greater long-term health complications. Heating and ventilation were inadequate in many prisons.

During the year the family of imprisoned Hoa Hao Buddhist and land rights activist Tran Thi Thuy reported prison officials at An Phuoc Prison in Binh Duong Province had repeatedly denied medical treatment for a tumor on her uterus and an open wound on her abdomen, despite repeated requests. Authorities reportedly told Thuy that she would not receive treatment unless she "confessed" to the crimes for which she was convicted. Police had taken Thuy to a police hospital in September 2015 and in March, but the hospital and prison officers reportedly refused to share Thuy's medical records with her family. Thuy's family reported that prison authorities forced her to work under poor conditions and stated family members experienced regular police harassment.

In March prisoners of conscience Tran Huynh Duy Thuc, Dinh Nguyen Kha, Tran Vu Anh Binh, and Lieu Ly conducted a 13-day hunger strike at Xuyen Moc prison in Ba Ria-Vung Tau Province to protest a prison rule prohibiting inmates from sharing food with each other and from sending and receiving documents to family members. On May 24, Tran Huynh Duy Thuc started a 14-day hunger strike to protest his transfer to a prison in Nghe An Province, significantly further from his family, and to demand a national referendum on the country's political system.

Serious health conditions exacerbated by poor or delayed medical care, forced prison labor, poor sanitation, and malnutrition caused most deaths in prison. Some prisoners' family members alleged death resulted from lethal force by authorities (see section 1.a.).

Prisoners generally were required to work but received no wages. Authorities placed prisoners in solitary confinement for standard periods of three months. Some political prisoners reported they experienced solitary confinement more frequently than nonpolitical prisoners. Prison authorities reportedly also placed some transgender individuals in solitary confinement due to confusion over whether to place them in male or female quarters. Ministry of Public Security officials often prohibited reading and writing materials, especially for political prisoners. Family members continued to make credible claims prisoners received extra food or other preferential treatment by paying bribes to prison officials.

Authorities typically sent political prisoners to specially designated prisons that also held regular criminals and, in many cases, kept political prisoners separate from nonpolitical prisoners. Authorities completely isolated some high-profile political prisoners. Activists reported Ministry of Public Security officials assaulted prisoners of conscience to exact confessions or used other means to induce written confessions, including instructing fellow prisoners to assault them or making promises of better treatment.

Some former and existing prisoners of conscience reported prisoners received insufficient food and that of poor quality. Several former prisoners reported they received only two small bowls of rice and vegetables daily, often mixed with foreign matter such as insects or stones.

Administration: There was no active system of prison ombudsmen, but the law provides for oversight of the execution of criminal judgments by the National Assembly, people's councils, and the CPV's Vietnam Fatherland Front (VFF), an umbrella group that oversees the country's government-sponsored social organizations.

Authorities limited prisoners to one 30-minute family visit per month and generally permitted family members to give various items, including money, supplemental food, and bedding to prisoners. Family members of political prisoners reported that prison authorities at times revoked visitation rights, often after political prisoners staged hunger strikes or refused to follow instructions. Family members also continued to report government surveillance and harassment by security officials as well as frequent interference with their work, school, and financial activities.

In contrast with normal practice for nonpolitical prisoners, authorities routinely transferred political prisoners to facilities far from their families, making it difficult for family members to visit them. On May 6, the Ministry of Public Security transferred prisoner of conscience Tran Huynh Duy Thuc from Xuyen Moc Prison in Ba Ria-Vung Tau Province to Detention Center 6 in Nghe An Province, nearly 1,000 miles away from his home and relatives in Ho Chi Minh City.

Religious leaders and former prisoners of conscience reported Ministry of Public Security officials did not permit prisoners to conduct religious services or receive visits by religious leaders. Family members and some former prisoners reported certain prison authorities did not permit prisoners to have religious texts while in detention.

Independent Monitoring: Local and regional International Committee of the Red Cross officials neither requested nor carried out prison visits during the year. The government did not allow foreign diplomats or domestic or foreign NGOs to conduct credible monitoring of prison conditions.

d. Arbitrary Arrest or Detention

The constitution states that a decision by a court or prosecutor is required for the arrest of any individual, except in the case of a "flagrant offense." The law allows the government to arrest and detain persons for significant periods of time under vague national security provisions of the penal code, such as the continued pretrial detention since 2015 of Nguyen Van Dai and Le Thu Ha for "conducting propaganda against the state" (article 88). The government continued to arrest and detain individuals for peacefully expressing political or religious views under other legal provisions of the penal code, including "causing public disorder" (article 245), "resisting persons on duty" (article 257), or "abusing democratic freedoms" (article 258). Authorities regularly subjected activists and suspected criminals to administrative detention or house arrest.

Role of the Police and Security Apparatus

The Ministry of Public Security is responsible for internal security and controls the national police, a special national security investigative agency, and other internal security units. Provincial and local-level police often maintained significant discretion in their activities. The Bureau of Investigation of the Supreme People's Procuracy (national-level public prosecutor's office) examines allegations of abuse by security forces. Four of 19 members of the Politburo were actual or former Ministry of Public Security officials, compared with three of 16 members of the previous Politburo. The government appointed existing and former Ministry of Public Security officials to a range of senior positions, including President Tran Dai Quang, Deputy Prime Minister Truong Hoa Binh, Chairman of the Office of the Communist Party Central Committee Nguyen Van Nen, Chief Justice of the Supreme People's Court Nguyen Hoa Binh, and Acting Chairman of the Government Committee on Religious Affairs Bui Thanh Ha. Former security officials also held key leadership positions in provincial-level government, including Hanoi People's Committee Chairman Nguyen Duc Trung and Thai Nguyen Province Party Secretary Tran Quoc To.

People's committees (the executive branch of local governments) had substantial authority over police forces and prosecutors at the provincial, district, and local levels. Although the Supreme People's Procuracy had authority to investigate security force abuse, police organizations operated with significant discretion, little transparency, and limited public oversight. Police officers sometimes acted with impunity. At the commune level, guard forces composed of residents or members of government-affiliated social organizations commonly assisted police. Police were generally effective at maintaining public order, but other police capabilities, especially investigative, were very limited. Police training and resources, particularly at the local level, were inadequate. Several foreign governments and international organizations continued to assist in training provincial police and prison management officials to improve their professional skills.

A variety of specialized government agencies oversee migration and border enforcement. The Ministry of Public Security's Department of Immigration Management is responsible for overseeing migration in and out of the country. The military performs public safety functions in border areas. The Ministry of Finance controls the customs agency, and other agencies oversee quarantine and other functions. The official responsibilities, jurisdictions, and command structures of these agencies vary considerably. Border control officers often lacked the capacity to identify and interdict illegal border movements such as trafficking in persons; narcotic drugs and precursor chemicals; and trafficking of wildlife, timber, and counterfeit goods.

Arrest Procedures and Treatment of Detainees

The law includes provisions related to arrest procedures and the treatment of detainees prior to case adjudication. Police and other investigative agencies usually executed warrants for arrest, custody, and temporary detention. By law police generally need a decision by the People's Procuracy to arrest a suspect, although in some limited cases they need a court decision. In most cases the People's Procuracy at the state, provincial, and district levels issued such arrest warrants. Under urgent circumstances, such as when evidence existed a person was preparing to commit a crime or when police caught a person in the act of committing a crime, police could make an arrest without a warrant. In such cases the People's Procuracy must issue a decision to approve or not to approve the arrest within 12 hours of receiving notice from police.

The People's Procuracy must issue a decision to initiate a formal criminal investigation of a detainee within three days of arrest; otherwise, police must release the suspect. The law allows the procuracy to request two additional three-day extensions allowing for an extension of the custody time limit to a maximum of nine days.

The law affords detainees access to counsel from the time of their detention, but authorities continued their use of bureaucratic delays to deny timely access to legal counsel. In cases investigated under national security laws, the government has the authority to prohibit access by defense lawyers to clients until after officials complete an investigation and formally charge the suspect with a crime.

By law authorities may keep individuals in detention pending investigation for up to 24 months, in four-month increments, for "especially serious offenses," including national security cases. During this period of detention, authorities have the discretion to deny family visits or access to counsel. In many such cases, authorities did not provide attorneys access to their clients or the evidence against them until immediately before the case went to trial and without adequate time to prepare their cases. On September 23, blogger Nguyen Huu Vinh stated at his appeals court trial that he learned about the trial only one day prior, from a prison guard. By law authorities must request the local bar association, legal aid center, or the VFF to appoint an attorney for criminal cases involving juveniles, individuals with mental or physical disabilities, and persons formally charged with capital crimes. The National Assembly passed a revised criminal procedure code in November 2015 but delayed its implementation during the year, pending additional revisions to the penal code.

The law requires authorities to inform persons held in custody, accused of a crime, or charged with a crime of their rights under the law, including the right to an attorney. Under most circumstances, once advised, the accused are responsible for obtaining their own attorney. The law obligates defense attorneys to begin the defense of their client from the time authorities issue custody decisions.

Authorities generally provided notification to consular offices of the arrest of foreign nationals but sometimes delayed that notification. Government officials usually provided consular access to arrested or detained foreign nationals but imposed strict conditions on this access, including requiring police and other government officials to be present during meetings between consular officers and the arrested foreign nationals and, on occasion, videotaping these meetings.

The law allows defense counsel to be present during interrogations of their clients. The law also requires authorities to give defense attorneys access to case files and permit them to copy documents. Attorneys were usually able to exercise these rights. Defense lawyers representing politically sensitive detainees reported significant difficulty carrying out their responsibilities and exercising their rights under the law. Many detainees reported limited access to materials and information that would assist in the preparation of their legal defense, including the penal code itself. This was especially the case for detainees held on national security charges.

Police generally informed families of detainees' whereabouts, but family members could visit a detainee only with the permission of the investigator. During the investigative period, authorities routinely denied detainees access to family members, especially in national security cases. Before a formal indictment, detainees have the right to notify family members, although the Ministry of Public Security held a number of detainees suspected of national security violations incommunicado. Time spent in pretrial detention counted toward time served upon conviction and sentencing.

Authorities continued to deny requests for family visitation to activist Le Thi Thu Ha since her arrest in December 2015. Authorities reportedly allowed the wife of activist Nguyen Van Dai to visit him for the first time on November 3, after Dai had spent nearly 11 months in pretrial detention. Authorities in Nha Trang city did not allow the mother of blogger Nguyen Ngoc Nhu Quynh (also known as Me Nam or Mother Mushroom) to visit her in pretrial detention following her October 10 arrest but allowed the mother to deliver food and clothing.

For crimes infringing on national security as well as some exceptionally serious offenses, courts may impose probation or administrative detention upon an individual for a period of one to five years after completion of the original sentence. Terms of the probation typically included confinement to a residence and deprivation of the right to vote, run for office, or perform government or military service.

As of June the country confined approximately 14,000 persons in "compulsory detoxification establishments" (previously referred to as "06" centers or "compulsory treatment institutions"). This was a decline from approximately 40,000 persons in 2008 (when authorities introduced methadone maintenance treatment). There were 123 centers, of which 39 were voluntary treatment centers (including methadone clinics), and the remainder were in the process of transitioning as part of a government initiative to reform the drug treatment system. The law requires a judicial proceeding before sending any individual to a compulsory detoxification establishment. Despite this legal requirement, judicial procedures were often perfunctory, did not occur in the formal judicial system, and "defendants" were not given legal counsel. Authorities continued to send sex workers who used drugs to compulsory detoxification establishments. The Ministry of Labor, Invalids, and Social Affairs (hereafter Ministry of Labor) estimated there was a high HIV prevalence rate of 13 percent in such centers. The law also specifies detainees in such establishments may work no more than three hours per day. There continued to be reports that forced labor occurred in at least some of these establishments.

The law allows for bail as a measure to replace temporary detention, but authorities infrequently used it. The law authorizes investigators, prosecutors, or courts to allow for the depositing of money or valuable property in exchange for bail.

<u>Arbitrary Arrest</u>: Arbitrary arrest and detention, particularly for political activists and individuals protesting land seizures or other injustices, remained a serious problem. Authorities subjected many religious and political activists to varying degrees of arbitrary detention in their residences, in vehicles, at local police stations, at "social protection centers," or local government offices. Officials also frequently detained human rights activists upon their return from overseas trips.

Police and plainclothes security officers detained or placed under house arrest numerous activists in the days leading up to the May 23-25 visit of a foreign leader to Hanoi and Ho Chi Minh City.

On May 24, plainclothes Ministry of Public Security and Hanoi police officers prevented human rights advocate Nguyen Quang A from meeting a foreign leader. The officers surrounded Quang A's residence to prevent him from leaving, and when Quang A attempted to leave, they forced him into an unmarked vehicle and drove him around the outskirts of the city for several hours. The officers released Quang A after it was clear he would not be able to attend the diplomatic event in time. On a separate occasion, security officials detained blogger and activist Pham Doan Trang at a hostel in Ninh Binh Province while she was on her way to meet the same foreign leader. On May 25, authorities in Ho Chi Minh City detained activist Tran Hoang Phuc at a police station for eight hours to prevent him from taking part in a youth event with a visiting foreign leader. Police reportedly searched his bag and confiscated his cell phone and personal documents.

On multiple occasions in May and June, Hanoi and Ho Chi Minh City police blocked activists from leaving their homes or detained them in social rehabilitation centers or "social support centers" to prevent or punish attendance at environmental demonstrations. On June 3, Hanoi City police reportedly confined activist and violinist Ta Tri Hai at a social rehabilitation center for sex workers, drug addicts, and homeless persons in Dong Anh District for two days.

On March 24, authorities released prisoner of conscience Dinh Tat Thang after a court in Thanh Hoa Province sentenced him to time served in pretrial detention (seven months and 11 days). In August 2015 police arrested Thang and charged him with "abusing democratic freedoms" for writing public letters criticizing provincial leaders and police.

On December 16, a Thai Binh Province court sentenced democracy activists and former prisoners of conscience Tran Anh Kim and Le Tranh Tung to 13 and 12 years in prison, respectively, with four years of additional probation for each. The court convicted both individuals for "carrying out activities aimed at overthrowing the people's administration" (article 79 of the penal code) for attempting to create a new political organization, "National Forces Raising the Democratic Flag."

Authorities also subjected many individuals who were not activists, particularly individuals suspected of crimes, to varying degrees of arbitrary detention. On January 11, police officials in Tinh Bac commune, Son Tinh District, Quang Ngai Province, detained Nguyen Tan Tam on allegations of theft without notifying his family or school. Police then searched Tam's house and belongings without a search warrant. Tam committed suicide two days later, leaving a letter stating he was innocent. Tam's family alleged that police had assaulted Tam while in custody and forced him to plead guilty. According to press, police began an investigation into the incident.

<u>Pretrial Detention</u>: The law defines four levels of crimes: less serious offenses, serious offenses, very serious offenses, and especially serious offenses. The allowable time for temporary detention during an investigation varies depending on the level of offense. Activists often reported some of these investigations exceeded these prescribed periods, which ranged from a maximum of four months for less serious offenses to 24 months for the most serious cases. Activists also reported police and prosecutors used lengthy periods of pretrial detention to punish or to pressure human rights defenders to confess to crimes.

In 2014 Ministry of Public Security officials arrested well-known activist blogger Nguyen Huu Vinh (also known as Anh Ba Sam) and his assistant Nguyen Thi Minh Thuy and charged them with "abusing democratic freedoms" (article 258 of the penal code). On March 23, a Hanoi court sentenced Vinh and Thuy to five and three years in prison, respectively, after they had served more than 22 months in pretrial detention, exceeding the maximum length permitted by law for their charges. On September 23, an appeals court upheld their sentences.

Authorities continued to hold activists Nguyen Van Dai and Le Thu Ha (since December 2015) in pretrial detention.

<u>Detainee's Ability to Challenge Lawfulness of Detention before a Court</u>: Persons arrested or detained often were not entitled to challenge in court the legal basis or arbitrary nature of their detention and obtain prompt release or compensation if detention is found to be unlawful.

<u>Amnesty</u>: The government released two prisoners of conscience under amnesty provisions. On May 17, authorities granted amnesty and early release to Catholic priest Nguyen Van Ly approximately three months before the end of his eight-year jail term. On October 7, authorities granted amnesty and early release to land rights activist Nguyen Kim Nhan two months before the end of his five and one-half-year jail term.

e. Denial of Fair Public Trial

The law provides for the independence of judges and lay assessors, but the judiciary was not strong and was vulnerable to influence by outside elements such as senior government officials and CPV leadership. During the year there were credible reports that political influence, endemic corruption, and inefficiency strongly distorted the judicial system. Most, if not all, judges were members of the CPV and underwent screening by the CPV and local officials during their selection process to determine their suitability for the bench. The party's influence was particularly notable in high-profile cases and other instances in which authorities charged a person with challenging or harming the party or state. Trial outcomes were largely predetermined in trials considered politically sensitive.

The law specifies that judges and people's assessors (trained laypersons who participate in hearings in socialist judicial systems) shall adjudicate independently; prohibits agencies, organizations, and individuals from interfering in trials; and provides that hearings shall be timely and public, that courts shall emphasize the principles of equality before the law and the adversarial process, and that authorities consider the accused innocent until proven guilty. There continued to be a shortage of well-trained and experienced lawyers (including defense lawyers) and judges.

Trial Procedures

The constitution states that all persons are equal before the law, that defendants are innocent until proven guilty, and that they have the right to a defense lawyer and a speedy public trial. The court uses an inquisitorial system, where the judge plays the primary role of asking questions and ascertaining facts in a trial. Prosecution and defense attorneys, and people's assessors play a limited role. The constitution contains a provision "guaranteeing the adversarial principle in trials," but the courts had not introduced adversarial procedures into the judicial system. The National Assembly passed a new criminal procedure code in November 2015 but delayed its implementation during the year. Defense lawyers routinely complained that in many of their cases, it appeared judges made a determination of guilt concerning the accused prior to conducting the trial. Trials generally were open to the public, but in sensitive cases judges closed trials or strictly limited attendance.

The People's Procuracy submits charges against an accused person and serves as prosecutor during trials. Defendants have the right to prompt, detailed information of the charges levied against them, but defendants did not always experience such treatment. Authorities generally upheld the rights of defendants to be present and have a lawyer at trial, although it was not necessarily the lawyer of their choice. The law stipulates that the spoken and written language of criminal proceedings is Vietnamese, but the state provides interpretation if participants in the criminal procedure use another spoken or written language. The government provided a lawyer to defendants unable to afford one only in cases involving a juvenile offender or someone with mental or physical disabilities, or with possible sentences of life imprisonment or capital punishment.

Defense lawyers routinely reported having little time before trials to talk to their clients or examine the evidence against their clients. Although the defendant or defense lawyer has the right to examine evidence and cross-examine witnesses, there were multiple instances in which neither defendants nor their lawyers had access to government evidence in advance of the trial, knowledge of which witnesses would be called, or the opportunity to cross-examine witnesses or challenge statements. A defendant has a right to present a defense, but the law does not expressly state that the defendant has the right to call witnesses. Judges presiding over politically sensitive trials often did not permit defense lawyers and defendants to exercise their rights under the law.

Police routinely interrogated suspects without their attorneys present, and there were many reports that investigators used physical abuse, isolation, excessively lengthy interrogation sessions, and sleep deprivation to compel detainees to confess. In national security cases, judges occasionally silenced defense lawyers who were making arguments on behalf of their clients in court. Convicted persons have the right to at least one appeal. District and provincial courts did not publish their proceedings, but the Supreme People's Court continued to publish the proceedings of all cases it reviewed.

On March 2, a court in Long An sentenced a 15-year-old boy, Nguyen Mai Trung Tuan, to 30 months in prison for "intentionally inflicting injury on state officials" (article 104 of the penal code). The court reportedly rejected the defense of nine lawyers who represented Tuan pro bono. Local authorities did not allow family members or supporters to enter the courtroom, and they detained activist Le Thi Em during the trial.

There continued to be credible reports that authorities pressured defense lawyers not to take religious or democracy activists as clients. Authorities also restricted, harassed, arrested, disbarred, and, in some cases, detained human rights attorneys who represented political activists. Authorities prohibited lawyers Le Tran Luat, Huynh Van Dong, Le Cong Dinh, Nguyen Van Dai, and Nguyen Thanh Luong from practicing law.

Political Prisoners and Detainees

The government held fewer political prisoners than in previous years due to completion of prison sentences and a trend toward shorter sentences for political prisoners. There were approximately 94 political prisoners as of December 16, compared with approximately 95 political prisoners at the end of 2015. The government asserted there were no political prisoners in the country and did not permit regular access to such persons by international human rights or humanitarian organizations.

During the year the government sentenced 12 activists for peacefully exercising internationally recognized human rights. The government convicted one individual for "causing public disorder" (article 245), three for "abusing democratic freedoms" (article 258), two for "carrying out activities aimed at overthrowing the people's administration" (article 79), and six for "conducting propaganda against the state" (article 88). In comparison, the government sentenced two activists in 2015.

Civil Judicial Procedures and Remedies

The 2013 constitution provides that any person illegally arrested and detained, charged with a criminal offense, investigated, prosecuted, brought to trial, or subjected to judgment enforcement illegally has the right to compensation for material and mental damages and restoration of honor. The law provides a mechanism for pursuing a civil action to redress or remedy abuses committed by authorities. Administrative and civil courts heard civil suits, with legal procedures being similar to criminal cases and using members of the same body of judges and people's assessors to adjudicate the cases. All three systems of courts--criminal, administrative, and civil--continued to be vulnerable to corruption and outside influence, lack of independence, and inexperience. Very few victims of government abuse sought or successfully received redress or compensation through the court system.

Although the law provides for a process for civil redress in cases of human rights violations by a civil servant, there was little effective recourse to civil or criminal judicial procedures to remedy human rights abuses, and few legal experts had relevant experience.

The government continued to prohibit class-action lawsuits against government ministries, thus rendering ineffective joint complaints from land rights petitioners.

Property Restitution

Widespread complaints persisted of inadequate or delayed compensation, official corruption, and a general lack of transparency and due process in the government's process of confiscating land and displacing citizens to make way for infrastructure projects. In 2014 a revised land law went into effect that makes some efforts to address challenges to land expropriation and provides improved procedural transparency. Many still complained the most worrisome clauses and principles remained. The revised law maintains considerable decision-making authority over land pricing, allocation, and land reclamation for local people's committees and people's councils, which many asserted contributed to unfair business practices and corruption. Furthermore, many contended that by allowing land seizures for socioeconomic development, as opposed to only for national defense and public welfare, the law fails to provide significant reform.

During the year there were numerous reports of clashes between local residents and authorities at land expropriation sites. Disputes over land expropriation for socioeconomic development projects remained a significant problem, causing public grievances. Many villagers whose land the government forcibly seized protested at government offices for failure to address their complaints. Some coercive land seizures resulted in violence and injuries to both state officials and villagers. There were also reports of suspected plainclothes officers or "thugs" hired by development companies intimidating and threatening villagers or breaking into activists' homes. Authorities arrested and convicted multiple land rights protesters on charges of "resisting persons on duty" or "causing public disorder."

In early 2015 local authorities in Ky Anh District, Ha Tinh Province, reportedly denied 155 Catholic students admission to schools near their homes and instructed them to go to schools much farther away. Parishioners alleged local officials tried to force them to leave their homes to seize their land for an economic development project. In July 119 of these students returned to neighborhood schools, and the provincial government directed local authorities to provide supplemental training to help the students catch up with others for the new school year, official press reported.

The number of complaints filed over land disputes increased dramatically in the last decade, constituting 70 to 90 percent of all petitions and complaints, according to government figures.

f. Arbitrary or Unlawful Interference with Privacy, Family, Home, or Correspondence

The law prohibits arbitrary interference with privacy, family, home, or correspondence, but the government did not consistently protect these rights, and authorities at times violated these rights.

By law security forces need public prosecutorial orders for forced entry into homes, but Ministry of Public Security agents and local police officers regularly chose not to follow proper procedures to obtain such orders in the cases of activists and instead asked residents' permission to enter homes with the threat of repercussions for failure to cooperate.

Authorities routinely physically prevented political activists and family members of political prisoners from meeting with foreign diplomats or traveling abroad. Tactics included setting up barriers or guards outside activists' residences and summoning individuals to local police stations (also see section 1.d).

On February 4, nearly 50 police officers and local officials, both in uniform and plainclothes, from Dong Da District, Hanoi, reportedly broke into the house of labor activist Le Thi Cong Nhan's mother after verbally reading, but refusing to provide a hard copy of, a search warrant. During the search police officers violently dragged Le Thi Cong Nhan and her sister Le Thi Minh Tam out of the house.

Throughout the year authorities reportedly sought to prevent human rights advocate Nguyen Quang A from meeting foreign officials. On June 2, plainclothes security officials in Hanoi prevented Quang A from meeting a visiting foreign delegation, forcing him into a vehicle, and driving him to a province near the border with China. On August 24, Bac Ninh Province authorities physically prevented Quang A from meeting a foreign diplomat. Local authorities placed a bulldozer in the middle of the street leading to the place where Quang A was staying.

Authorities opened and censored targeted private mail; confiscated packages and letters; and monitored telephone conversations, e-mail, text messages, blogs, and fax transmissions. The government cut telephone lines and interrupted cell phone and internet services of a number of political activists and their family members.

The Ministry of Public Security maintained a system of household registration and block wardens to monitor unlawful activity. While this system was less intrusive than in the past, the ministry closely monitored individuals engaged in, or suspected of engaging, in unauthorized political activities. Family members of activists widely reported incidents of physical harassment, intimidation, and questioning by ministry officials. Such harassment included denying jobs or business opportunities to family members of former or existing prisoners of conscience.

On multiple occasions in January and February, plainclothes police officers in Lam Dong Province reportedly attacked human rights activist and Catholic former prisoner of conscience Tran Minh Nhat and his family members with stones, causing head injuries to multiple individuals. Throughout January to April, local police reportedly also verbally threatened his family members, prevented him from travelling to receive medical treatment, burned his crops, killed his livestock, and sprayed his house with pesticides.

The government continued to encourage couples to have no more than two children. While the law does not prohibit or provide penalties for those having more than two children, some CPV members reported informally administered repercussions, including restrictions on job promotion (see section 6, Women).

CPV membership remained a prerequisite to career advancement for nearly all government and government-linked organizations and businesses. Nevertheless, economic diversification continued to make membership in the CPV and CPV-controlled mass organizations less essential for financial and social advancement.

Section 2. Respect for Civil Liberties, Including:

a. Freedom of Speech and Press

The constitution and law state that citizens have the right to freedom of speech and freedom of the press. The government continued, however, to use broad national security and antidefamation provisions to restrict these freedoms. The law defines the crimes of "sabotaging the infrastructure of socialism," "sowing divisions between religious and nonreligious people," and "propagandizing against the state" as serious offenses against national security. It also expressly forbids "taking advantage of democratic freedoms and rights to violate the interests of the state and social organizations."

Freedom of Speech and Expression: The government continued to restrict speech that criticized individual government leaders; criticized the party; promoted political pluralism or multiparty democracy; or questioned policies on sensitive matters, such as human rights, religious freedom, or sovereignty disputes with

China. The government also sought to impede criticism by monitoring meetings and communications of journalists and activists, including in academic institutions.

In August, Hanoi police reportedly detained on multiple occasions Nguyen Van Dien, a member of the Vietnam Path movement, and twice forcibly returned him to his hometown in Yen Bai Province after he rode a bicycle around Hanoi while wearing a shirt with the slogans "Spratly and Paracel islands belong to Vietnam."

On March 30, the Ho Chi Minh City People's Court sentenced Nguyen Dinh Ngoc (also known as Nguyen Ngoc Gia) to four years in prison and three years of probation for writing articles critical of the state for *Dan Lam Bao* and *Dan Luan* blogs in 2014.

The government tolerated limited debate about sensitive political or social topics. It allowed limited discussion in the press and among civil society and religious organizations about key proposed laws at the National Assembly level, such as the draft Law on Belief and Religion, which was passed on November 18, and the draft Law on Associations, which was postponed for further review.

Press and Media Freedoms: The CPV, government, and party-controlled mass organizations exercised legal authority over all print, broadcast, online, and electronic media primarily through the Ministry of Information and Communications, under the overall guidance of the CPV Propaganda and Education Commission. Private ownership or operation of any media outlet remained prohibited, but there were widespread reports of subcontracting to private establishments. Media independent of government authority operated on a limited basis online, primarily via blogs and social media, but independent journalists faced government harassment.

The law allows for the government to punish publishers if they publish "untruthful information" in the fields of statistics; atomic energy; management of prices, charges, fees, and invoices; education; civil aviation; vocational training; hydrometeorology; cartography; and health.

The law limits satellite television access to senior officials, foreigners, luxury hotels, and the press, but persons throughout the country continued to be able to access foreign programming via home satellite equipment or cable. Cable television, including foreign-origin channels, was widely available to subscribers in urban areas.

The government permitted foreign-based outlets (including, but not limited to, the BBC and CNN), although the law requires foreign television broadcasts to run on a 30- to 60-minute delay to enable content monitoring. In practice such channels ran on a 10-minute delay. Viewers reported obstruction of various commentaries, documentaries, and movies on human rights incidents in the country, the Vietnam War, the Cold War, the Soviet era, or events in China.

Major foreign media outlets reported the government refused to issue visas for reporters who previously covered sensitive political topics, particularly reporters for overseas Vietnamese-language press. Foreign reporters also reported authorities turned them away at airports even if they had valid entry visas.

Violence and Harassment: There continued to be a significant number of reports of security officials attacking, threatening, or arresting journalists and independent bloggers because of their coverage of sensitive stories.

In August police confirmed that former editor in chief of newspaper *Nguoi Cao Tuoi* Kim Quoc Hoa (also known as Nguyen Quoc Hoa) was free on bail and awaiting investigation. Authorities penalized Hoa for allegedly running a series of investigative articles criticizing the corruption and wrongdoing of high-ranking state officials. In May 2015 authorities charged him with "abusing democratic freedoms" (article 258 of the penal code).

On October 10, police in Nha Trang city arrested blogger Nguyen Ngoc Nhu Quynh (also known as Me Nam or Mother Mushroom), charged her with "conducting propaganda against the state" (article 88 of the penal code), and continued to hold her incommunicado in pretrial detention as of the end of the year. On May 15, a plainclothes female police officer in Ho Chi Minh City reportedly beat Quynh and dragged her into a police car, preventing her from taking part in an environmental demonstration. Authorities detained her for 24 hours and subsequently transferred her to her home in Khanh Hoa Province during the night.

On November 2, Ho Chi Minh City police arrested blogger Ho Van Hai and accused him of spreading information and documents on the internet that were against the government, according to media. Police issued a statement stating Hai may have violated article 88 of the penal code ("conducting propaganda against the state"). Four days later police in Ho Chi Minh City arrested activist bloggers Luu Van Vinh and Nguyen Van Duc Do and charged them with "carrying out activities aimed at overthrowing the people's administration" (article 79 of the penal code).

Foreign journalists noted they continued to be required to notify authorities about travel outside Hanoi when it was to an area considered sensitive, such as the Northwest or Central Highlands, or involved a story the government otherwise might consider sensitive. Numerous foreign journalists reported harassment by security officials, including threats not to renew their visas if they continued to publish stories on "sensitive" topics.

During the visit of a foreign leader in mid-May, authorities ordered a BBC team to halt reporting, reportedly in retaliation for the BBC team meeting with a prominent human rights advocate earlier in the week.

Censorship or Content Restrictions: The Ministry of Information and Communications and the CPV Propaganda and Education Commission frequently intervened directly to dictate or censor a story. Propaganda officials forced editors for major press outlets to meet regularly to discuss what topics were off-limits for reporting. More often pervasive self-censorship due to the threat of dismissal and possible arrest enabled the party and government to control media content. The government continued its practice of penalizing journalists for failing to self-censor, to include revoking journalists' press credentials.

In May and June, the Ministry of Information and Communications and party officials penalized Mai Phan Loi, head of the Hanoi Bureau of the *Ho Chi Minh City Legal Affairs* newspaper, for meeting a visiting foreign leader and for traveling abroad without permission. Loi's employer summoned him for questioning less than two weeks after he met the foreign leader. On June 20, the ministry revoked Loi's press credentials, criticizing him for posting a controversial poll on Facebook regarding recent accidental crashes of Vietnamese Navy aircraft. On June 23, Loi's newspaper fired him. Activists noted that the government aimed to penalize Loi for his advocacy for greater press freedom.

In September the party's Propaganda and Education Commission directed that news outlets suspend coverage of a major steel industrial project in Ninh Thuan Province to prevent public criticism in the wake of an environmental disaster caused by pollution from a steel plant earlier in the year, according to press.

The law tightly restricts press freedom. Decree 159/2013/ND-CP stipulates fines of 70 million to 100 million Vietnamese dong (VND) ($3,140 to $4,500) for journalists, newspapers, and online media that publish or broadcast information deemed harmful to national interests. The decree authorizes the government to fine journalists and newspapers. The decree establishes fines ranging from five million to 10 million VND ($225 to $450) for journalists who fail to cite their sources of information and for journalists and newspapers that "use documents and materials from organizations and personal letters and materials from individuals."

Government regulations authorize the information ministry to revoke licenses of foreign publishers, and each foreign publisher must reapply annually to maintain its license. Nonetheless, street peddlers and shops oriented to tourists openly sold foreign-language editions of some banned books. Foreign-language periodicals were widely available in cities, but the government occasionally censored articles.

Internet Freedom

The government continued to exercise various forms of control over internet access. It allowed access to the internet but only through a limited number of internet service providers (ISPs), all of which were fully or substantially state-controlled companies. Despite these controls, internet access and usage continued to grow. According to Internet Live Stats, 52 percent of the population had access to the internet in 2016.

Authorities continued to suppress online political expression through politically motivated arrests and convictions of bloggers as well as through short-term detentions, surveillance, intimidation, and illegal confiscations of computers and cell phones of activists and family members. The government continued to use national security and other vague provisions of the penal code against activists who peacefully expressed their political views online. Political dissidents and bloggers reported the Ministry of Public Security routinely ordered disconnection of their home internet service.

The government sometimes blocked websites it deemed politically or culturally inappropriate, including sites operated by overseas Vietnamese political groups. The government additionally blocked the websites of Radio Free Asia, Voice of America, and the BBC Vietnamese news service. State-owned ISPs routinely blocked domestic Vietnamese-language websites that contained content criticizing the CPV or promoting political reform. Some domestic subscribers reported using workarounds, such as virtual private networks, to access blocked sites.

Facebook reported it had 42 million users countrywide. In general authorities did not block access to the site, which gave citizens a space for free and open debate and dialogue. On multiple occasions throughout the year, however, authorities temporarily blocked Facebook to prevent activists from organizing protests over a major fish kill in the central region of the country linked to industrial pollution. The government also monitored Facebook posts and punished activists who used the internet to organize protests.

On August 23, a court in the Khanh Hoa Province sentenced Nguyen Huu Quoc Duy and Nguyen Huu Thien An to three and two years of prison, respectively, for "conducting propaganda against the state" (article 88 of the penal code). Authorities charged Duy with creating a Facebook group to "slander the government." Duy's family members reported the court refused to let them visit Duy, send food packages, or provide their own defense lawyer. An was charged with spray-painting an obscenity on the side of a police building and for attending a human rights training event. Duy and An were both associated with the "Zombie Movement," an online group that formed in 2015 with inspiration from an anticommunist rap song.

The Ministry of Information and Communications required all internet companies, social networking sites, and websites that provided information or commentary about "politics, economics, culture, and society" based in the country to register and obtain an operating license. The ministry also required such owners to submit detailed plans of their content and scope for approval. It used administrative sanctions such as fines and suspensions of operating permits to regulate online activity, including decrees 159 and 174 under the Law on the Handling of Administrative Violations.

Decree 72/2013/ND CP requires all companies and organizations operating websites providing content on "politics, economics, culture, and society" or social networks, including blogging platforms, to register with the government. Under the decree such companies and organizations must locate at least one server in the country to facilitate requests for information from the government and store posted information for 90 days and certain metadata for up to two years. In 2014 the government issued a circular that further outlines the guidelines and implementation of Decree 72. Social network and blog users are required to provide their full name, national identification number, and address before creating an account. According to the circular, in-country general website and social network operators must allow authorities to inspect local servers upon request and must have a mechanism to remove prohibited content within three hours of detection or notification by authorities. During the year representatives of the internet startup community criticized these regulations, which the government had not yet begun enforcing.

During the year the Ministry of Information and Communications issued new regulations restricting media organizations' use of Facebook forums, which provided users a space for open discussion and debate. On June 26, Document No. 816/PTTH&TTDT required provincial-level offices to increase supervision of websites and social media pages, including those managed by news outlets. Document No. 779/CBC-TTPC, issued July 1, requires that news outlets review their social media pages to prevent user comments aimed at "propaganda and distortion." This document specifies that newspaper senior staff are responsible for any failures to censor social media content under the control of the media organization.

On September 6, the Ministry of Information and Communications revoked the press credentials of Infonet journalist Luong Tan Huong and Dan Tri ("Intellectual") journalists Pham Phuc Hung, Le Trinh Truong, and Nguyen Dinh Hung for failing to properly moderate their news organizations' Facebook forums.

The government forbids direct access to the internet through foreign ISPs, requires domestic ISPs to store information transmitted on the internet for at least 15 days, and requires ISPs to provide technical assistance and workspace to public security agents to allow them to monitor internet activities. The Ministry of Public Security has long required "internet agents," including cybercafes, to register the personal information of their customers, to store records of internet sites visited by customers, and to participate in government investigations of online activity. Internet cafes continued to install and use government-approved software to monitor customers' online activities. The Ministry of Public Security enforced these and other requirements and monitored selectively.

Academic Freedom and Cultural Events

Foreign academic professionals temporarily working at universities in the country could discuss nonpolitical topics widely and freely in classes, but government observers regularly attended classes taught by both foreigners and nationals. The government continued to require international and domestic organizations to obtain approval to host conferences involving international sponsorship or participation in advance.

The government continued to prohibit any public criticism of CPV and state policy, including by independent scientific and technical organizations, even when the criticism was for a purely academic audience.

Although the government controlled art exhibits, music, and other cultural activities, it continued to allow artists broader latitude to choose themes for their works. Authorities continued to restrict public art displays and musical performances through requirement of substantial permission procedures. The government allowed universities more autonomy over international exchanges and cooperation programs, but visa requirements for visiting scholars and students remained onerous.

Many activists reported Ministry of Public Security officials threatened university leaders if they did not expel activists from their respective universities, although their political activities were peaceful. Multiple activists also reported academic institutions refused to allow them to graduate due to their human rights advocacy.

On March 20, police in Ho Chi Minh City briefly detained Professor Pham Minh Hoang and 14 students for taking part in a course in which he taught the history of civic rights in the country.

b. Freedom of Peaceful Assembly and Association

Freedom of Assembly

Although the constitution affords individuals the right to assemble, local authorities routinely inhibited assembly, and the government continued to restrict and monitor all forms of public protest or gathering. Law and regulations require persons wishing to gather in a group to apply for a permit, which local authorities issued or denied without explanation. Only those arranging publicized gatherings to discuss sensitive matters appeared to require permits, and persons routinely gathered in informal groups without government interference. The government generally did not permit demonstrations perceived to be political. The government also restricted the right of certain religious groups, both registered and unregistered, to gather for worship.

The Ministry of Public Security and local police routinely prevented activists from peacefully assembling. There were numerous reports of police dispersing gatherings of anti-China activists, land rights advocates, human rights defenders, bloggers and independent journalists, and former prisoners of conscience. On March 22, one day before the trial of bloggers Nguyen Huu Vinh (also known as Anh Ba Sam) and Nguyen Thi Minh Thuy, the ministry made public a new decree,

Circular 13/2016/TT-BCA, which allows security forces to detain individuals gathering or protesting outside of courthouses during trials.

On February 27, authorities in Hanoi, Ho Chi Minh City, and other major cities dispersed peaceful demonstrations held by victims of land seizures and other perceived government injustices in commemoration of the "International Day for Vietnam Land Petitioners." Police reportedly assaulted multiple demonstrators, held them in police custody for hours, and forcibly transported them far away from town centers.

In mid-July authorities prevented multiple demonstrations to celebrate the Permanent Court of Arbitration's July 12 ruling in favor of the Philippines, and against China, concerning certain issues in the South China Sea. Local authorities in Duong Noi village, Hanoi, reportedly detained multiple land rights protesters, including Dang Bich Phuong, Truong Van Dung, and Nguyen Thuy Hanh, when they sought to join the demonstrations.

On February 20-22, local security forces in Ba Ria-Vung Tau Province reportedly harassed individuals attending a cybersecurity training session organized by Reporters Without Borders and Defend the Defenders at Saigon-Binh Chau Resort. Harassment included questioning organizers about permits, verbally threatening participants, cutting power to the conference site, pressuring the hotel to terminate the event contract, and entering the event room and forcing the gathering to disperse.

On March 30, a court in Ho Chi Minh City sentenced land rights activists Ngo Thi Minh Uoc, Nguyen Thi Be Hai, and Nguyen Thi Tri to four, three, and three years in prison, respectively, with two years of probation for each. In 2014 police charged them with "conducting propaganda against the state" (article 88 of the penal code) after they staged a demonstration in Ho Chi Minh City demanding that the government return seized land to farmers and criticizing government corruption, China, and CPV slogans.

The government typically allowed groups to assemble for meetings on nonsensitive issues and on occasion allowed larger sensitive gatherings. In August hundreds of persons participated in Pride Walk events for Viet Pride in Hanoi and Ho Chi Minh City. In July and August, local authorities in Nghe An and Phu Yen Provinces largely allowed thousands of Catholics to participate in environmental demonstrations and volunteer activities to press the government to address fish deaths caused by an industrial spill.

Freedom of Association

The constitution affords individuals the right of association, but the government continued to restrict freedom of association severely and neither permitted nor tolerated opposition political parties. The government prohibited the establishment of private, independent organizations, insisting that persons work within established, party-controlled mass organizations, usually under the aegis of the VFF. Some entities, including unregistered religious groups, operated outside of this framework with little or no government interference, and authorities demonstrated some increased tolerance of independent NGOs. Some registered organizations, including governance and environment-focused NGOs, reported increased scrutiny of their activities due to leadership transitions, the May National Assembly election, and an environmental disaster in the central region in April.

The country's legal and regulatory framework codifies the primacy of the CPV and establishes mechanisms for restricting freedom of NGOs to act and organize, including restricting freedom of association, assembly, expression, and the press. The government used complex and politicized registration systems for NGOs and religious organizations to suppress unwelcome political and religious participation. Despite these restrictions, the number of independent NGOs continued to grow throughout the year.

Laws and regulations governing NGOs restrict their ability to engage in policy advocacy or conduct research outside of state-sanctioned topics. Decision 97, for instance, which took effect in 2009, prohibits organizations focused on social science and technology from operating in fields such as economic policy, public policy, political issues, and a range of other areas considered sensitive. Authorities also do not permit them to engage in the public distribution of policy advocacy positions.

On March 3, authorities in Ho Chi Minh City prevented the League of Independent Vietnamese Writers from holding its first literary awards ceremony. Local authorities pressured the owner of the venue to withdraw permission, forcing the writers to move the ceremony to a private residence. Authorities also prevented several prominent writers and intellectuals, including Do Trung Quan, Bui Chat, Le Phu Khai, Pham Dinh Trong, and Nguyen Dang Hung, from attending the ceremony.

c. Freedom of Religion

See the Department of State's *International Religious Freedom Report* at
www.state.gov/religiousfreedomreport/.

d. Freedom of Movement, Internally Displaced Persons, Protection of Refugees, and Stateless Persons

The constitution provides for freedom of internal movement, foreign travel,
emigration, and repatriation, but the government imposed some limits on the
movement of certain individuals, especially those convicted under national security
or related charges or those outspoken in their criticism of the government. The
government generally cooperated with the Office of the UN High Commissioner
for Refugees (UNHCR) and other humanitarian organizations in providing
protection and assistance to internally displaced persons, refugees, returning
refugees, asylum seekers, stateless persons, and other persons of concern.

The government allowed UNHCR fact-finding and monitoring visits, but local
authorities closely monitored all aspects of such visits. Some members of ethnic
minority groups who fled the Central Highlands for Cambodia or Thailand, some
reportedly due to religious persecution, asserted that upon their return, Vietnamese
authorities detained and questioned them, sometimes for up to several days.
Family members also reported police closely monitored both those who had fled to
Cambodia and Thailand, and their relatives.

In-country Movement: Several political dissidents, amnestied with probation or
under house arrest, were officially restricted in their movements. These included
Le Cong Dinh, Nguyen Phuong Uyen, Nguyen Tien Trung, and Dinh Nhat Uy.
The Ministry of Public Security continued to monitor and selectively restrict the
movement of prominent activists Nguyen Dan Que, Nguyen Bac Truyen, Pham Ba
Hai, Pham Chi Dung, Nguyen Hong Quang, Nguyen Ngoc Nhu Quynh, Pham
Minh Hoang, Thich Khong Tanh, Duong Thi Tan, Tran Minh Nhat, and Tran Thi
Nga, among many others. Many activists reported they resorted to deceptive
tactics to avoid travel restrictions. Several activists reported authorities had
confiscated their national identification cards, preventing them from traveling
domestically by air and from conducting routine administrative matters. Other
activists and religious leaders reported increased freedom of in-country movement
compared with previous years.

Some activists reported authorities prevented them and their family members from
leaving their homes during politically sensitive events (see also section 1.d.).

On April 17, Hanoi authorities reportedly prevented members of the Independent Journalist Association of Vietnam from meeting at a coffee shop to discuss the upcoming visit of a foreign leader. Plainclothes police blocked members Nguyen Tuong Thuy and Vu Quoc Ngu from departing their homes. Police also detained members for different reasons to prevent their attendance; police detained Pham Chi Dung at the Giang Vo police station, ostensibly for a traffic violation, and authorities detained Bui Minh Quoc at Kim Lien police station to discuss his residential registration.

On May 20, police in Ho Chi Minh City reportedly assaulted and detained for two days former prisoner of conscience Nguyen Viet Dung at Cau Kho ward police station, in District 1. Police forced Dung to return to Nghe An Province on May 22. As soon as he landed in Vinh, the capital of Nghe An Province, local police forced him into a vehicle and assaulted and interrogated him. Local police officials later returned him to his home in Yen Thanh district, Nghe An Province. Ministry of Public Security and police officials reportedly took these actions to prevent Dung from meeting a visiting foreign leader in Ho Chi Minh City.

A government restriction regarding travel to certain areas required citizens and resident foreigners to obtain a permit to visit border areas, defense facilities, industrial zones involved in national defense, areas of "national strategic storage," and "works of extreme importance for political, economic, cultural, and social purposes."

Local police required citizens to register when staying overnight in any location outside of their own homes; the government appeared to enforce these requirements more strictly in some Central and Northern Highlands districts. Foreign passport holders must also register to stay in private homes, although there were no known cases of local authorities refusing to allow foreign visitors to stay with friends and family. There were multiple reports of police using the excuse of "checking on residency registration" to intimidate and harass activists and prevent them from traveling outside of their place of registration (see sections 1.c., 1.d., and 1.f.).

In general authorities did not strictly enforce residency laws, and migration from rural areas to cities continued unabated. Moving without permission, however, hampered persons seeking legal residence permits, public education, and health-care benefits.

<u>Foreign Travel</u>: Prospective emigrants occasionally encountered difficulties obtaining a passport; authorities regularly confiscated passports, at times indefinitely. There were multiple reports of individuals who fled abroad via the land borders with Laos or Cambodia because they were unable to obtain passports or exit permission.

The Ministry of Public Security continued to use foreign travel prohibitions against certain activists and religious leaders. Authorities banned and prevented dozens of individuals from traveling overseas or entering the country, withheld their passports on vague charges, or refused to issue passports to certain activists or religious leaders without clear explanation.

Although their probation or prison terms ended, the government continued to prohibit Le Quoc Quan, Nguyen Khac Toan, Pham Ba Hai, Pham Hong Son, Le Thi Kim Thu, Nguyen Hong Quang, and other former prisoners of conscience from receiving a passport and traveling overseas. Authorities also refused to issue passports to the family members of certain activists, including the wife of former prisoner of conscience Le Quoc Quan.

In July and August, authorities at Tan Son Nhat Airport in Ho Chi Minh City separately stopped pastor Pham Ngoc Thach and lawyer Le Cong Dinh and banned them from traveling abroad to attend a human rights conference.

On September 28, authorities at Noi Bai Airport in Hanoi banned Defend the Defenders' leader Vu Quoc Ngu from traveling to a Reporters Without Borders meeting in Paris, citing national security and social order reasons.

Other individuals temporarily detained or harassed upon return from travel abroad included activist Nguyen Anh Tuan; human rights advocate Mai Van Tam; and Vu Minh Khanh, the wife of detained human rights lawyer Nguyen Van Dai.

Activists and religious leaders reported multiple instances where security authorities had issued passports and allowed foreign travel after refusing to do so for many years. In these instances, however, police required that travelers report on their activities abroad upon their return to Vietnam.

<u>Emigration and Repatriation</u>: The government generally permitted citizens who emigrated to return to visit, but police denied entry visas to and sometimes deported some foreign-based political activists. Ministry of Public Security officials made clear that prisoners of conscience who received temporary

suspended sentences to allow for their relocation abroad could have their sentences reimposed if they attempted to return to Vietnam.

Protection of Refugees

Access to Asylum: The law does not provide for the granting of asylum or refugee status, and the government has not established a system for providing protection to refugees.

Refoulement: According to international human rights NGOs, the government pressured Cambodia and Thailand to return members of Central Highlands ethnic minority groups who had fled to Cambodia or Thailand seeking refugee status and protection from harassment and restrictions on religious freedom by Vietnamese officials. NGOs also reported that Vietnamese security officials, including provincial security agents from Gia Lai Province, visited Bangkok and contacted asylum seekers via Facebook to monitor them and pressure them to return to Vietnam.

In November 2015 a UNHCR spokesperson expressed concern about reports that authorities arrested nine North Korean nationals in October and subsequently transferred them to China, where they were at risk of deportation to North Korea. The spokesperson noted that, if repatriated, the individuals would be at risk of very serious human rights violations.

Stateless Persons

Authorities reported that by 2013 they had naturalized nearly all of the 10,000 individuals who had been stateless and previously resident in Cambodia. UNHCR officials estimated that fewer than 200 persons awaited final approval by the government at year's end. The government also continued to work to restore citizenship for approximately 800 stateless women who had lost Vietnamese nationality after moving abroad to marry foreigners but had subsequently returned to Vietnam upon losing their foreign citizenship (in many cases due to divorce).

Section 3. Freedom to Participate in the Political Process

The constitution provides the ability to elect directly representatives to the National Assembly, people's councils, and other state agencies. Under the law National Assembly elections take place once every five years by secret ballot. Although the constitution provides that one may vote at age 18 and run for election to the

National Assembly or People's Council at age 21, the ability of citizens to change their government democratically was severely limited. The CPV screened all candidates through a process overseen by the Vietnam Fatherland Front (VFF).

The law requires minimums for the percentage of final candidates for election to the National Assembly who are ethnic minorities (18 percent) and women (35 percent) and to the provincial-level people's councils who are women (35 percent). The law allows individuals in custody and temporary detention as well as those who are undergoing compulsory educational and drug treatment to vote during elections. The law prohibits individuals who have lost specific "political rights," typically due to a criminal conviction, from voting or running for office.

Elections and Political Participation

<u>Recent Elections</u>: The most recent elections to select members of the National Assembly, in May, allowed limited competition among CPV-vetted candidates but were neither free nor fair. The CPV's VFF chose and vetted all candidates through an opaque, multistage process. CPV candidates won 475 of the 496 seats. The remaining 21 were non-CPV candidates unaffiliated with any party. There were no candidates from a party other than the CPV. The national election committee later disqualified two candidates, one for having dual nationality and another due to a corruption investigation, leaving 494 total National Assembly members at the end of the year.

According to the government, 99 percent of eligible voters cast ballots in the May election, a figure activists and international observers considered improbably high. Voters may cast ballots by proxy, and officials charged local authorities with assuring that all eligible voters cast ballots by organizing group voting and verifying that all voters within their jurisdiction had voted. There were numerous reports throughout the country that election officials had stuffed ballot boxes and artificially ensured high turnout.

The law allows citizens to "self-nominate" as National Assembly candidates and submit applications for the VFF election vetting process. In the months leading up to the May National Assembly elections, an informal coalition of legal reformers, academics, activists, and human rights defenders attempted to register as self-nominated, non-CPV, "activist independent" candidates. In contrast to the party's candidates, these candidates actively used Facebook and social media to advertise their policy platforms. VFF officials refused, however, to allow any activist independent candidates to make the final ballots, and authorities instructed official media to criticize certain activist independent candidates. According to press reports, the VFF allowed two self-nominated candidates on final ballots, but both individuals were party members.

The National Assembly, although largely composed of CPV members, continued to take incremental steps to assert itself as a legislative body and sponsored multiple open forums to debate laws related to human rights and religious freedom.

<u>Political Parties and Political Participation</u>: Chapter I, article 4 of the revised constitution outlines the political role of the CPV. While the article does not detail specific constitutional powers, section 1 asserts the party's role as "vanguard of the working class and of the Vietnamese nation" and the "leading force in the state and society," a broad role not given to any other constitutional entity. Section 2 further references the party's responsibility to the public. Section 3 states that "all Party organizations and members of the Communist Party of Vietnam operate within the framework of the constitution and the laws." The CPV Politburo functioned as the supreme decision-making body, although technically it reported to the CPV Central Committee. Political opposition movements and other political parties were illegal. Authorities did not permit NGOs to monitor the election process.

The government continued to restrict severely public debate on and criticism of the one-party state. Some groups and individuals, however, openly called for permitting multiparty democracy. Critics discussed the pros and cons of human rights-related laws and provisions, including revisions to the penal code, criminal procedures code, and the new draft laws on associations, access to information, demonstrations, and religion and belief. They also discussed other sensitive political issues, including rights for lesbian, gay, bisexual, transgender, and intersex persons; land rights; and environmental issues.

<u>Participation of Women and Minorities</u>: The law requires 35 percent of final candidates for the National Assembly and provincial people's councils to be women and 18 percent of final candidates for the National Assembly to be from minority groups. There were 132 women (approximately 27 percent) in the National Assembly; one female minister in the 27-member cabinet; three women in the 19-member Politburo, one of whom was ethnic Thai minority; and four women on the 15-member Supreme People's Court. Ethnic minorities held 86 seats (approximately 17 percent) in the National Assembly; there was one male minority minister in the cabinet, and no ethnic minorities on the Supreme People's Court.

Section 4. Corruption and Lack of Transparency in Government

The law provides criminal penalties for corruption by officials; however, the government generally did not implement the law effectively, and officials often engaged in corrupt practices with impunity. There were numerous reports of government corruption during the year.

Corruption: Corruption continued to be a major problem despite government leaders' continued focus on the issue throughout the year. The 2015 Vietnam Provincial Governance and Public Administration Performance Index released on August 8 noted that nepotism and bribery in the public sector were prevalent throughout the country, including in the public education, health-care, construction, and government employment sectors. The country's Provincial Competitiveness Index stated that nearly half (46 percent) of foreign companies cited corruption as their greatest challenge. Corruption also continued to be a problem in land allocation, bidding for construction and infrastructure projects, and official development assistance. In July the World Bank announced it had debarred Thanh Loi Group for four years for misrepresenting bids for two separate projects.

During the year the government's new leaders initiated new investigations into former administration officials, including former Minister of Industry and Trade Vu Huy Hoang and businesses associated with former Prime Minister Nguyen Tan Dung's daughter, Nguyen Thanh Phuong. The government also initiated an investigation into corruption at PetroVietnam Construction (PVC), a state-owned enterprise. In September authorities arrested four executives of the company and issued a warrant for Trinh Xuan Thanh, a former PVC chairman, National Assembly member, and deputy chairman of the People's Committee (provincial government) of Hau Giang Province. During the last administration, high-profile corruption cases almost exclusively had focused on the banking sector.

On July 19, the Ho Chi Minh City People's Court sentenced Vietnam Construction Bank former chairman Pam Cong Danh to 30 years in prison in connection with a nine trillion VND ($405 million) economic loss to the bank caused by corruption.

Corruption among police remained a significant problem at all levels, and police sometimes acted with impunity. Internal police oversight structures existed but were subject to political influence. Transparency International's 2013 Global Corruption Barometer found the police force to be the country's most corrupt institution.

A 2013 anticorruption law allows citizens to complain openly about inefficient government, administrative procedures, corruption, and economic policy, but authorities prohibited attempts to organize disaffected citizens, with corruption protest organizers subjected to arrest and harassment.

Financial Disclosure: The anticorruption law requires senior government officials and National Assembly members to disclose their income and assets and explain changes from the previous year's disclosure. In 2014 the Politburo issued a directive requiring improved asset declaration by officials holding managerial positions. Additionally, supervisors have the right to question an employee's disclosure. While the law does not stipulate a penalty for noncompliance, a 2014 decree provides for possible reprimand, warning, suspension, or removal for noncompliant civil servants.

In 2015 the government reported 99 percent of government workers disclosed their finances. Media still questioned the government's capacity to verify tax returns for its approximately one million workers and highlighted examples of civil servants driving fancy cars or sending children to study overseas on small official salaries. A Government Inspectorate of Vietnam project to create a publicly accessible database including civil servant salaries and properties remained stalled.

Public Access to Information: The constitution states that citizens have the right to access information. In accordance with the law, the *Official Gazette* published most government legal documents in its daily editions but not party documents such as Politburo decrees. Most government agencies maintained websites in both Vietnamese and English, as did the National Assembly. Decisions of the Supreme People's Court Council of Judges were generally accessible through the court's website, although it was difficult for individuals to obtain government information.

Members of the public were able to review budget implementation estimates, which were preliminary numbers within the government's proposed budget. The public could not review the government's executive budget proposal prior to final approval.

Section 5. Governmental Attitude Regarding International and Nongovernmental Investigation of Alleged Violations of Human Rights

The government did not permit independent, local human rights organizations to form or operate, nor did it tolerate attempts by organizations or individuals to criticize its human rights practices publicly. The government used a wide variety of methods to suppress domestic criticism of its human rights policies, including surveillance, detention, prosecution and imprisonment, interference with personal communications, and limits on exercise of the freedoms of speech, press, and assembly. The government occasionally allowed representatives of international human rights organizations to visit the country but usually strictly controlled their itineraries (see section 1.b.).

Section 6. Discrimination, Societal Abuses, and Trafficking in Persons

Women

<u>Rape and Domestic Violence</u>: The law prohibits using or threatening violence against women or taking advantage of a person who cannot act in self-defense. It also criminalizes rape, including spousal rape. The law subjects rapists to two to seven years' imprisonment. In severe cases of rape, including organized rape, a repeat offense, or extreme harm to a victim, sentences may range from seven to 15 years' imprisonment. Authorities prosecuted rape cases fully, but the government did not release arrest, prosecution, conviction, or punishment statistics.

Authorities treated domestic violence cases as civil cases, unless the victim suffered injuries involving more than 11 percent of the body. The law specifies acts constituting domestic violence, assigns specific portfolio responsibilities to different government agencies and ministries, and stipulates punishments for perpetrators ranging from warnings and probation to imprisonment for three months to three years.

Domestic violence against women was common. In March, Hanoi Medical University researchers reported the results of a survey in a district of Hanoi showing that 35 percent of pregnant women were victims of domestic violence, mostly at the hands of their husbands. In November 2015 NGOs released two surveys on violence against women and girls. One survey reported 59 percent of married women had suffered physical or sexual abuse at least once in their lives, typically from a male partner or member of the family. Another study revealed 83 percent of women and girls in Hanoi and 91 percent of those in Ho Chi Minh City had experienced at least one form of sexual harassment during their lives. Respondents who were students reported they experienced instances of whistling and teasing, while office worker respondents reported harassment via e-mail and text messages. According to the survey, most harassment occurred on the street.

NGOs and survivor advocates considered many of the legal provisions against domestic violence weak, and the government did not release arrest, prosecution, conviction, or punishment statistics. Social stigma prevented many victims from coming forward, due to fear of harassment from their spouses or family. Officials acknowledged domestic violence as a significant social concern, and the media discussed it openly. While police and legal systems generally remained unequipped to deal with cases of domestic violence, the government, with the help of international and domestic NGOs, continued to train police, lawyers, community advocates, and legal system officials in the law.

Several domestic and international NGOs worked to address domestic violence. Domestic NGOs operated hotlines for victims in major cities. The Center for Women and Development, supported by the Women's Union, also operated a nationwide hotline, but it was not widely advertised in rural areas. Although rural areas often lacked the financial resources to provide crisis centers and hotlines, a law establishes "reliable residences" to allow women to turn to another family while local authorities and community leaders attempt to confront the alleged abuser and resolve complaints. There were 300 such residences in the country, all established through the Women's Union at the commune level.

According to a 2015 UN Women Access to Justice report, many remote villages used informal mediation to resolve cases of domestic violence. Often these mediations did not conform to law and resulted in both parties receiving blame, rather than just the perpetrator. Rather than confront social and family stigma as well as economic uncertainty, many women remained in abusive marriages.

The government, with the help of international NGOs, continued to support workshops and seminars aimed at educating women and men about domestic violence and women's rights and highlighted the problem through public awareness campaigns. The government continued to implement a national action plan to prevent and combat domestic violence through 2020. Local NGOs affiliated with the Women's Union remained engaged on women's concerns, particularly violence against women and trafficking of women and children.

Sexual Harassment: The law prohibits sexual harassment in the workplace. Publications and training on ethical regulations for government and other public servants did not mention the problem of sexual harassment.

Victims of sexual harassment may contact social associations such as the Women's Union to request their involvement. Victims with access to a labor union representative may file complaints with union officers. In serious cases victims may sue offenders under a provision that deals with "humiliating other persons" and specifies punishments that include a warning, noncustodial reform for up to two years, or a prison term ranging from three months to two years. Nevertheless, there were no known prosecutions or sexual harassment lawsuits, and most victims were unwilling to denounce offenders publicly.

<u>Reproductive Rights</u>: The constitution stipulates that society, families, and all citizens implement "the population and family planning program." The law affirms an individual's right to choose contraceptive methods; access gynecological diagnosis, treatment, and check-ups during pregnancy; and obtain medical services when giving birth at health facilities. The government generally enforced these provisions.

The law states that couples or individuals have the right to give birth to one or two children, with exceptions based on government decree. There is no legal provision punishing citizens who have more children than the stipulated number.

The CPV and certain ministries and localities issued their own regulations, applying only to CPV members and government officials, regarding family size. A decree issued by the Politburo subjects CPV members to reprimand if they have three children, removes them from a ranking position if they have four children, and expels them from the CPV if they have five children. Violating the decree also decreases the likelihood of promotion and may lead to job termination. The CPV did not enforce these provisions consistently.

The Population and Reproductive Health Strategy for 2011-20 applies to all citizens and strives to maintain the average number of children per reproductive-age couple at 1.8. The government, primarily through broad media campaigns, maintained its strong encouragement of family planning.

<u>Discrimination</u>: The law provides for gender equality in all aspects of life, but women continued to face societal discrimination. Despite the large body of law and regulation devoted to the protection of women's rights in marriage and the workplace, as well as provisions that call for preferential treatment, women did not always receive equal treatment in employment, education, or housing, particularly in rural areas.

Gender gaps in education declined, but certain gaps remained. According to a 2013 UN Women-funded report, professional qualifications of female workers were lower than those of male workers. There were substantial differences in the education profile of men and women at postsecondary level. The number of female students enrolled in higher education applied technology programs was much smaller than the number of men enrolled.

Another UN-funded report on social protection for women and girls noted that female migrants working in nonofficial sectors had difficulties accessing standard housing. These women resided in temporary accommodations that were unsafe and lacked basic services.

Although the law provides for equal inheritance rights for men and women, women continued to face cultural discrimination. A son was more likely to inherit property than was a daughter, unless otherwise specified by a legal document. A study conducted in 2014 showed women had less information than men on land access and that a cultural preference for sons over daughters for inheritance was still prevalent, despite the legal mandate that all citizens have equal rights.

The Women's Union and the government's National Committee for the Advancement of Women continued to promote women's rights, including political, economic, and legal equality, and protection from spousal abuse. The Women's Union also operated microcredit consumer-finance and other programs to promote the advancement of women. The government's 2011-20 National Strategy Plan for Gender Equality asserts that men and women should have substantive equality in opportunity, participation, and benefits in the political, economic, cultural, and social domains. As of year's end, however, there was no financial commitment from the government for the implementation of the national program on gender equality for 2016-20. The government passed requirements for gender-based budgeting as part of the budget law for the year.

Gender-biased Sex Selection: According to the Ministry of Health, the national average male-female sex ratio at birth for the first half of the year was 113.4 to 100. The government acknowledged the problem, highlighted reduction of the ratio as a goal in the national program on gender equality, and continued to take steps to address it. In October 2015 the Ministry of Health launched a joint campaign with the UN Population Fund to address the imbalance.

Children

Birth Registration: By law the government considers anyone born to at least one citizen parent to be a citizen, although persons born to non-Vietnamese parents may also acquire citizenship under certain circumstances. Parents did not register all births immediately, sometimes due to a lack of incentive or knowledge of the requirement. The law requires a birth certificate to access public services, such as education and health care, and the choice by some parents, especially ethnic minorities, not to register their children affected their ability to enroll them in school and receive government-sponsored health care.

Education: Education is compulsory, tuition free, and universal through age 14, although many families were required to pay a variety of school fees. Under a government subsidy program, ethnic-minority students were exempt from paying school fees. Nevertheless, authorities did not always enforce the requirement or enforce it equally for boys and girls, especially in rural areas, where government and family budgets for education were limited, and children's contributions as agricultural laborers were valuable.

Child Abuse: Experts at a Ministry of Labor and the UN Children's Fund (UNICEF) seminar in April reported 8,200 recorded cases of child abuse across the country between 2011 and 2015, according to official media. Experts at the seminar criticized the government for its lax punishment of violators. NGOs noted the difficulty of obtaining accurate data on the prevalence of child and adolescent sexual abuse, which may be underreported.

On April 4, the government and UNICEF established a new Family and Juvenile Court in Ho Chi Minh City to address the specific needs of children during legal consultations. This court is a model court that the government stated it intended to replicate throughout the country.

Early and Forced Marriage: The legal minimum age of marriage is 18 for girls and 20 for boys, and the law criminalizes organizing marriage for, or entering into marriage with, an underage person.

Sexual Exploitation of Children: Sexual exploitation of children under age 16 is illegal. The law criminalizes all acts of sale or deprivation of liberty of children as well as all acts related to child prostitution and forced child labor. Sentences range from three years' to life imprisonment, and fines range from five million to 50 million VND ($225 to $2,250). The law also specifies prison sentences for acts related to child prostitution, including harboring prostitution (12 to 20 years), brokering prostitution (seven to 15 years), and buying sex with minors (three to 15 years). The law similarly prohibits all acts of cruel treatment, humiliation, abduction, sale, and coercion of children into any activities harmful to their healthy development and provides for the protection and care of disadvantaged children.

The minimum age of consensual sex is 18. Statutory rape is illegal and may result in life imprisonment or capital punishment. Penalties for sex with minors between the ages of 16 and 18, depending upon the circumstances, vary from five to 10 years in prison. The penalty for rape of a child between ages 13 and 16 carries a sentence of imprisonment from seven to 15 years. If the victim becomes pregnant, the rape is incestuous, or the offender is in a guardianship position to the victim, the penalty increases to 12 to 20 years' imprisonment. The law considers all cases of having sexual intercourse with children less than 13 years of age rape of children, with sentences including 12 to 20 years' imprisonment, life imprisonment, or capital punishment. The government enforced the law, and convicted rapists received harsh sentences. The production, distribution, dissemination, or selling of child pornography is illegal and carries a sentence of three to 10 years' imprisonment.

Displaced Children: Media reported that approximately 21,000 children lived on the streets and sometimes experienced police harassment or abuse.

International Child Abductions: The country is not a party to the 1980 Hague Convention on the Civil Aspects of International Child Abduction. See the Department of State's *Annual Report on International Parental Child Abduction* at www.travel.state.gov/content/childabduction/en/legal/compliance.html.

Anti-Semitism

There were small communities of Jewish foreigners in Hanoi and Ho Chi Minh City, and there were no reports of anti-Semitic acts.

Trafficking in Persons

See the Department of State's *Trafficking in Persons Report* at www.state.gov/j/tip/rls/tiprpt/.

Persons with Disabilities

The constitution provides for the protection of persons with mental and physical disabilities. The law prohibits discrimination against or mistreatment of persons with physical and mental disabilities, encourages their employment, and requires equality for them in accommodation, access to education, employment, health care, rehabilitation, local transportation, and vocational training. The government continued to increase coordination with foreign governments, international organizations, NGOs, and private companies to review legal provisions governing implementation of the treaty, conduct feasibility studies, share international best practices, conduct informational workshops, promote the hiring of persons with disabilities, and hold awareness activities.

While the law requires that the construction of new or major renovations of existing government and large public buildings include access for persons with disabilities, enforcement continued to be sporadic, particularly for projects outside of major cities. The Ministry of Construction maintained units to enforce barrier-free codes and provide training on construction codes for inspectors and architectural companies in more than 22 provinces. Some new buildings and facilities in large urban cities included ramps and accessible entries. During the year the Ministry of Transportation's Civil Aviation Authority installed elevators and accessibility improvements in six airports and started developing additional services for passengers with disabilities.

Access to education for children with disabilities, particularly deaf children and those with intellectual disabilities, remained extremely limited. The Ministry of Education and Training estimated 500,000 children with disabilities had some access to education at the primary, secondary, and tertiary levels.

The law promotes and encourages the employment of persons with disabilities; however, social and attitudinal barriers remained problems.

There is no legal restriction on the right to vote for persons with disabilities, although many polling stations were not accessible, especially to persons with physical disabilities.

While the provision of social services to persons with disabilities remained limited, the government made some efforts to support the establishment of organizations of persons with disabilities and consulted them in the development or review of national programs, such as the National Poverty Reduction Program, vocational laws, and various educational policies. The National Coordination Committee on Disabilities, the Vietnam Federation on Disability, and their members from various ministries continued to work with domestic and foreign organizations to provide protection, support, physical access, education, and employment. The government operated a small network of rehabilitation centers to provide long-term, inpatient physical therapy. Several provinces, government agencies, and universities had specific programs for persons with disabilities.

As a result of the country's accession to the UN Convention on the Rights of Persons with Disabilities (CRPD) in February 2015, the government increased consultations and cooperation with NGOs and disabled persons organizations, including on preparing the country's first CRPD report. NGOs reported they continued to face challenges applying for funding for disability-related programs from provincial governments.

National/Racial/Ethnic Minorities

The law prohibits discrimination against ethnic minorities, but societal discrimination against ethnic minorities was longstanding and persistent. Local officials in some provinces, notably in the highlands, acted in contravention of national laws and discriminated against members of ethnic and religious minority groups. Despite the country's significant economic growth, the economic gap between many ethnic minority communities and ethnic Vietnamese (Kinh) communities persisted, although ethnic minority group members constituted a sizable percentage of the population in certain areas, including the Northwest and Central Highlands and portions of the Mekong Delta. Ethnic minority populations also experienced significant health challenges; indicators such as maternal and child mortality were significantly higher in ethnic minority areas, in comparison with urban and coastal areas.

International human rights organizations continued to allege authorities harassed and intimidated members of certain ethnic minority groups, including highlanders collectively described as "Montagnards" and ethnic minority Christians, in the Central Highlands. There were multiple reports that members of these ethnic minority groups fled to Cambodia and Thailand, seeking refugee status and claiming to be the victims of religious persecution. The government claimed these individuals were illegal migrants who left Vietnam in pursuit of economic opportunities. Human rights groups alleged the government pressured Cambodia and Thailand to refuse to grant these individuals refugee or temporary asylum-seeker status and to return them to Vietnam.

The government implemented policies in regions with significant ethnic minority populations through three interagency committees, the steering committees for the Northwest Region, the Central Highlands, and the Southwest Region. The government also continued to monitor certain highland minorities closely, particularly several ethnic groups in the Central and Northwest Highlands.

Authorities continued to imprison, using national security provisions of the penal code and with lengthy prison sentences, multiple ethnic minority individuals allegedly connected to overseas organizations the government claimed espoused separatist aims. In addition, activists often reported an increased presence of Ministry of Public Security agents during sensitive occasions and holidays throughout the region.

The government continued to attempt to address the socioeconomic gap between ethnic minority and ethnic Kinh communities through special programs to subsidize education and health facilities and expand road access and electrification of rural communities and villages. The government also continued to allocate land to ethnic minorities in the Central Highlands through a special program.

The law provides for universal education for children regardless of religion or ethnicity, and members of ethnic minority groups were not required to pay regular school fees. The government operated special schools for ethnic minority children, and there were 300 boarding schools for them in 50 provinces, mostly in the Northwest and Central Highlands and the Mekong Delta, including at the middle- and high-school levels, plus special admission and preparatory programs as well as scholarships and preferential admissions at the university level. The government also worked with local officials to develop local-language curricula, but it appeared to implement this program more comprehensively in the Central Highlands and the Mekong Delta and only in limited areas of the Northwest Highlands. There were also a few government-subsidized technical and vocational schools for ethnic minorities.

The government broadcast radio and television programs in ethnic minority languages in some areas. The government required ethnic-majority (Kinh) officials assigned to areas populated predominantly by ethnic minorities to learn the language of the locality in which they worked. Provincial governments continued initiatives designed to increase employment, reduce the income gap between ethnic minorities and ethnic Kinh, and make officials sensitive and receptive to ethnic minority cultures and traditions.

The government granted preferential treatment to domestic and foreign companies that invested in highland areas populated predominantly by ethnic minorities. The government also maintained infrastructure development programs that targeted poor, largely ethnic-minority areas and established agricultural extension programs for remote rural areas.

The National Assembly's Ethnic Minority Council, along with provincial ethnic minority steering committees, continued to support infrastructure development and address some problems related to poverty reduction and an increase in literacy rates.

Acts of Violence, Discrimination, and Other Abuse Based on Sexual Orientation and Gender Identity

The law does not address discrimination based on sexual orientation or gender identity. Societal discrimination and stigma continued to decrease but remained common, and local media reported general harassment of transgender individuals, including those in custody.

No laws criminalize consensual same-sex sexual conduct. In November 2015 the National Assembly passed a revised civil code with new provisions legalizing transgender individuals' right to change their sex, access health care, and change their gender identity.

In August nearly 1,000 individuals participated in Pride Walk for Viet Pride in Ho Chi Minh City, and there were Viet Pride celebrations held in 22 cities and provinces, including a bike rally with hundreds of riders in Hanoi.

HIV and AIDS Social Stigma

The law provides for the protection of specific rights of persons with HIV/AIDS, including for voluntary testing; confidentiality; the right to education, work, health care, and nondiscrimination; and mechanisms for legal redress in the event of any rights violations.

According to the 2015 Stigma Index study, 11.2 percent of persons with HIV, 16.6 percent of female sex workers, 15.5 percent of persons who inject drugs, and 7.9 percent of men who have sex with men reported having experienced rights violations within the 12 months prior to the survey. Multiple Indicator Cluster Surveys taken in 2014 showed stigma and discrimination against HIV-positive persons was widespread, with approximately 70 percent of female respondents reporting having faced some form of stigma and discrimination. Individuals with HIV continued to face barriers accessing and maintaining employment, with 4.2

percent of respondents reporting loss of jobs or income and 6.7 percent reporting prospective employers having refused them employment or job opportunities.

There were no official reported figures for access to HIV treatment or medication-assisted treatment for substance abuse disorders among detainees, most notably at compulsory detoxification centers. As of June the country maintained 14,000 persons in the system of "compulsory detoxification establishments" that, by the Ministry of Labor's conservative estimate, had a HIV-prevalence rate of 13 percent (also see section 1.d.).

Section 7. Worker Rights

a. Freedom of Association and the Right to Collective Bargaining

The constitution affords the right to association and the right to demonstrate but limits the exercise of these rights, including preventing workers from organizing or joining independent unions of their choice. While workers may choose whether to join a union and at which level (local or "grassroots," provincial, or national), the law requires every union to be under the legal purview and control of the country's only trade union confederation, the Vietnam General Confederation of Labor (VGCL).

The law gives the VGCL exclusive authority to give legal recognition to unions and confers on VGCL upper-level trade unions the responsibility to establish workplace unions. The Statutes of Vietnamese Trade Unions (SVTU), which is the VGCL's charter, establishes the VGCL as the head of the multilevel unitary trade union structure and carries the force of law. The law also stipulates that the VGCL answers directly to the CPV's VFF, which does not protect trade unions from government interference in or control over union activity.

The law also limits freedom of association by not allowing trade unions the legal right to have full autonomy in the administration of their affairs. The Trade Union Law subjects all workers' organizations to the organizational structures and rules prescribed by the SVTU, confers on the VGCL the rights and responsibilities of ownership over trade-union property (including the property and capital of all affiliate unions and contributions from union members), and gives the VGCL the right to represent lower-level unions. The law also allows for appointments of trade union leaders and officials, rather than elections by union members.

The law requires that where a workplace trade union does not exist, an "immediate upper-level trade union" must perform the tasks of a grassroots union, even where workers have not so requested or have voluntarily elected not to organize. Such tasks include negotiating collective bargaining agreements and other workplace rules and regulations, participating in the resolution of labor disputes, and engaging in social dialogue and other cooperation with employers. For nonunionized workers to organize a strike, they must request that the strike "be organized and led by the upper-level trade union," and if nonunionized workers wish to bargain collectively, the upper-level VGCL union must represent them. Neither the law nor related regulations specify the process for workers to request such representation or the minimum number of workers required to make such a request. Only Vietnamese citizens may form or join labor unions by law.

The VGCL has the responsibility for educating workers on their rights and obligations, representing workers (the "labor collective") in collective bargaining and individual workers' disputes, holding and leading legal strikes, and working with state agencies on labor relations, occupational health and safety, and other matters. Union dues are mandatory by law for union members and domestic and foreign employers. Union members pay 1 percent of their salary to the union, and employers pay 2 percent for every employee, regardless of whether they are a union member.

Collective labor disputes over rights must go through a conciliation council and, if the council does not resolve the matter, to the chair of the district-level people's committee. The law allows trade unions and employer organizations to facilitate and support collective bargaining and requires companies to establish a mechanism to enable management and the workforce to exchange information and to consult on subjects that affect working conditions. Regulations require conducting workplace dialogues every three months.

The law stipulates that trade unions have the right and responsibility to organize and lead strikes, and it establishes certain substantive and procedural restrictions on strikes. Strikes that do not arise from a collective labor dispute or do not adhere to the process outlined by law are illegal. The law makes a distinction between "interest-based" ("a dispute arising out of the request of the workers' collective on the establishment of a new working condition, ...in the negotiation process between the workers' collective and the employers") and "rights-based" ("a dispute between the workers' collective with the employer arising out of different interpretation and implementation of provisions of labor laws, collective bargaining agreements, internal working regulations, other lawful regulations and agreements") disputes. In contravention of international standards, the law forbids strikes over "rights-based" disputes. This includes strikes arising out of economic and social policy measures that are not a part of a collective negotiation process, as they are both outside the law's definition of protected "interest-based" strikes.

The law prohibits strikes by workers in businesses that serve the public or that the government considers essential to the national economy, defense, public health, and public order. "Essential services" is defined to include enterprises involved in electricity production; post and telecommunications; maritime and air transportation, navigation, and management; public works; and oil and gas production. The law also grants the prime minister the right to suspend a strike considered detrimental to the national economy or public safety. Essential services for which strikes may be restricted are generally limited to those for which a strike would endanger the public's safety or health.

The law prohibits strikes among workers across different employers, resulting in a ban on sector and industry-level protests and prohibits workers and unions from calling for strikes in support of multiemployer contracts. The law states that the executive committee of a trade union may issue a decision to go on strike only when at least 50 percent of workers support it.

Laws stipulate an extensive and cumbersome process of mediation and arbitration before a lawful strike over an interest-based collective dispute may occur. Before workers may hold a strike, they must submit their claims through a process involving a conciliation council (or a district-level labor conciliator where no union is present). If the two parties do not reach a resolution, unions must submit claims to a provincial arbitration council. Unions (or workers' representatives where no union is present) have the right either to appeal decisions of provincial arbitration councils to provincial people's courts or to strike. The law also stipulates strikers may not be paid wages while they are not at work. The law prohibits retribution against strikers. By law individuals participating in strikes declared illegal by a people's court and found to have caused damage to their employer are liable for damages. Individual workers may take cases directly to the people's court system, but in most cases they may do so only after conciliation has been attempted and failed.

Provisions of the penal code have the potential to suppress union activity. For example, national security-related article 89 states that "[t]hose who intend to oppose the people's administration by inciting, involving and gathering many people to disrupt security, oppose officials on public duties, obstruct activities of agencies and/or organizations… shall be sentenced to between five and 15 years of imprisonment." Under the same article, accomplices face between two and seven years of imprisonment.

The laws include provisions that prohibit antiunion discrimination and interference in union activity. The laws do not distinguish between workers and managers, however, and fail in prohibiting employers' agents, such as managers who represent the interests of the employer, from participating or interfering in union activity or provide sufficiently dissuasive sanctions for employer interference. Decree No. 95/2013/ND-CP on "administrative sanctions for violations in labor area," for example, limits applicable sanctions to fines only, and no specific remedies are available.

In October 2015 the government issued Decree 88 regarding administrative sanctions for interference in trade union activities. It specifically imposes fines of between three and 10 million VND ($135-$450) for discrimination against employees who establish or join a trade union or carry out trade union activities, and for any actions that disadvantage the operations of a trade union.

On June 19, the Hai Phong Economic Zone Trade Union and five Korean manufacturing enterprises based in Trang Due Economic Zone signed the country's first multienterprise collective bargaining agreement negotiated between a group of foreign-invested enterprises and trade unions to decide basic conditions of work, including recognition of union rights. The agreement would likely benefit nearly 2,500 workers through improved recruitment and female worker policies, increased base wages, better bonuses, allowances, leave, and rest time as well as conditions for ensuring trade union operations in the enterprises.

The VGCL reported 177 strikes from January through July, approximately the same level as the same period of 2015. Of those strikes, 69 percent were in foreign direct-investment companies (mainly Korean, Taiwanese, and Japanese companies). None of the strikes followed the authorized conciliation and arbitration process, and thus authorities considered them illegal "wildcat" strikes. The government took no action against the strikers and, on occasion, actively mediated agreements in the workers' favor. In some cases the government imposed heavy fines on those employers, especially foreign-owned companies that engaged in illegal practices leading to strikes.

A July 2015 report of the International Labor Organization (ILO) and International Finance Corporation's Better Work Vietnam program noted 62 percent of factories discriminated against or interfered in the activities of the trade union. Similarly, the data revealed that management staff continued to sit on trade union executive committees in approximately 45 percent of factories, which could undermine the function of the union as a legitimate representative voice for the workforce. At the same time, the report noted 7 percent of factories had cases of direct and overt management interference in union activities, and fewer still (eight employers had actually "tried" to interfere) were found to have prevented workers from meeting without management present. There were also credible reports employers used short-term or probationary contracts to avoid certain legally mandated worker benefits, such as unemployment insurance, or to inhibit workers from joining unions.

Multiple international labor NGOs collaborated with the VGCL to provide training to VGCL-affiliated union representatives on labor organizing, collective bargaining, and other trade union issues. Through its participation in an ILO industrial relations program, the VGCL engaged in a new form of bottom-up, worker-centered approach to organizing workers rather than having VGCL leaders determine when and where to form a union. This effort resulted in the formation of multiple new grassroots-established and -led trade unions, including four new unions at four of the Trang Due Economic Zone enterprises that signed the multienterprise collective bargaining agreement in June.

Because it is illegal to establish or seek to establish labor unions independent from the VGCL, there were no government-sanctioned domestic labor NGOs involved in labor organizing. Local labor NGOs, however, supported efforts to raise awareness of worker rights and occupational safety and health issues and to support internal and external migrant workers.

Labor activists and representatives of independent (non-VGCL) worker organizations faced antiunion discrimination. Independent labor activists seeking to form unions separate from the VGCL or inform workers of their labor rights sometimes faced government harassment. On January 17, authorities at Tan Son Nhat Airport in Ho Chi Minh City reportedly detained activist Hoang Duc Binh, a member of the independent labor rights organization Viet Labor Movement, for 10 hours and confiscated his passport, cell phone, and laptop. Authorities pressured him to renounce his membership in Viet Labor and later issued him a notice banning traveling overseas due to security reasons.

b. Prohibition of Forced or Compulsory Labor

The constitution and law prohibit forced or compulsory labor. The labor code's definition of forced labor, however, does not explicitly include debt bondage. The penal code does not establish a specific offense concerning forced labor, and the decree on administrative sanctions does not provide any penalty for violation of the labor code provisions prohibiting forced labor. A government circular prescribes punishments of between three and 10 years' imprisonment for labor trafficking. There were no prosecutions of forced labor cases during the year.

NGOs continued to report the occurrence of forced labor of men, women, and children within the country (see also section 7.c.).

Labor recruitment firms, most of which were affiliated with state-owned enterprises, and unlicensed brokers reportedly charged workers seeking international employment higher fees than the law allows, and they did so with impunity. Those workers incurred high debts and were thus more vulnerable to forced labor, including debt bondage.

Also see the Department of State's *Trafficking in Persons Report* at www.state.gov/j/tip/rls/tiprpt/.

c. Prohibition of Child Labor and Minimum Age for Employment

The constitution prohibits "discriminatory treatment, forced labor or the employment of people below the minimum working age." The law defines underage employees as anyone under age 18. Enterprises hiring children between 15 and 18 years of age are responsible for taking care of the underage employee in terms of "labor, salary, health, and education" in the labor process. The law prohibits children under 18 from working heavy, hazardous, and dangerous jobs. The law limits children between 15 and 18 to working a maximum of eight hours per day and 40 hours per week. Children between ages 13 and 15 may work only in light jobs (as defined by the Ministry of Labor), and considerations must be made for schooling, working conditions, labor safety, and hygiene. The law permits children to register at trade training centers, a form of vocational training, from age 14 without parental consent. While the law generally prohibits the employment of children under 13, it allows those under 13 to engage in specific types of work, as regulated by the ministry.

The labor ministry is responsible for enforcing child labor laws and policies. Government officials may fine and, in cases of criminal violations, prosecute employers who violate child labor laws. As part of the government's 2016-20

National Plan of Action for Children and National Program for Child Protection, the government continued efforts to prevent child labor and specifically targeted children in rural areas, disadvantaged children, and children at risk of exposure to hazardous work conditions.

The government's 2012 national child labor survey, published in 2014, indicated child labor was a significant problem and estimated there were more than 2.8 million economically active children in the country, of whom 1.75 million were child laborers as defined by the survey. The survey defined child labor as children engaged for more than one hour a day or five hours in a week for children ages five to 11, more than four hours a day or 24 hours in a week for children ages 12 to 14, or more than seven hours a day or 42 hours in a week for children ages 15 to 17.

Broadly defined, 60 percent of child labor was in agriculture, 22 percent in the service sector, and 18 percent in construction and manufacturing. The results of the survey indicated that children were engaged in child labor in the cultivation or production of a variety of goods, including cashews, coffee, fish, footwear, furniture, leather, pepper, rice, rubber, sugarcane, tea, textiles, timber, and tobacco. Of the 1.75 million child laborers, 85 percent were in rural areas and 15 percent in urban areas. Approximately 60 percent of child laborers were male. The survey reported 52 percent of child workers had dropped out of school, and only 24 percent were from households that fell below the country's poverty level. Moreover, 38 percent of child workers were from households with incomes twice the poverty threshold. The report also stated nearly 569,000 child laborers (approximately 32 percent) worked an average of more than 42 hours per week. Of these children, 96 percent did not attend school.

There were reports of children ages 10-18, and some as young as six, working under conditions of forced labor producing garments. The most recently available information from government raids, NGOs, and media reports indicated that groups of children were laboring in small, privately owned garment factories and informal garment workshops. Reports indicated that these employers were beating or threatening the children with physical violence. In addition, there was evidence that children as young as age 12 were working while confined in government-run rehabilitation centers. Employers forced these children to sew garments without pay under threat of physical or other punishments.

The ILO began implementation of the "Enhancing the National Capacity to Prevent and Reduce Child Labor Project" in partnership with the labor ministry. The project conducted awareness-raising campaigns, partnered with the government to build capacity, and plans to provide direct services to address child labor in the garment and agriculture sectors. International and domestic NGOs noted successful partnerships with provincial governments to implement national-level policies combatting child labor.

d. Discrimination with Respect to Employment and Occupation

The law prohibits multiple forms of discrimination in employment, labor relationships, and work but not explicitly in "all aspects of employment and occupation." The law prohibits discrimination based on gender, race, disability, color, social class, marital status, belief, religion, HIV status, and for membership in a trade union or participation in trade union activities. The law promotes and encourages the employment of persons with disabilities.

By law an enterprise may not dismiss a female employee who is engaged to be married or is pregnant, on maternity leave, or caring for a child less than one year of age unless the enterprise closes. The law prohibits women's employment in 77 categories of work, including work that is regularly underwater, in mines, or is harmful to "child-bearing and parenting functions." Employers may not compel female employees who are at least seven months' pregnant or who care for a child under one year of age to work overtime, at night, or in locations distant from their homes. The law requires equal pay for equal work in principle. The law prohibits sexual harassment in the workplace; however, according to the ILO, the legal provisions are not specific and potentially difficult to implement.

The law does not prohibit discrimination based on political opinion, age, language, national origin, sexual orientation, or gender identity. Moreover, no laws prohibit employers from asking about family status, to include intentions to marry or to start or raise a family, during job interviews, which could lead to employment discrimination, especially against women.

The government did not effectively enforce laws related to employment discrimination. Violations of employment discrimination provisions of the law include fines, including administrative fines of up to 50 to 75 million VND ($2,250 to $3,360) for violations of sexual harassment prohibitions. Penalties were not sufficient, however, to deter violations of employment discrimination. The government took some action to address employment discrimination against persons with disabilities. Companies with a workforce composed of at least 51 percent employees with disabilities may qualify for special government-subsidized loans.

Discriminatory hiring practices existed, including discrimination related to gender, age, and marital status. Women in the public sector were expected to retire at age 55, with the exception of women at ministerial rank or those with doctoral degrees or professors, compared with age 60 for men. Female-led enterprises accounted for an estimated 25 percent of the more than 300,000 enterprises. Female-led enterprises continued to have limited access to credit and international markets and inadequate knowledge in operation and financial management, in addition to the burden of social and family responsibilities. The law prohibits gender-based discrimination against employees performing work of equal value, but a woman's average hourly salary was only an estimated 80 percent of that of her male counterpart.

The law prohibits gender-based preferential hiring for jobs; although NGOs concluded such discrimination occurred, allegations were hard to prove. Social and attitudinal barriers and limited access to the workplace remained problems in the employment of persons with disabilities.

e. Acceptable Conditions of Work

The labor code governs all matters related to employment and employment relationships, including wages, hours of work, and occupational safety and health. By law the National Wages Council, which consists of representatives from the Ministry of Labor, VGCL, and the Vietnam Chamber of Commerce and Industry, determines regional minimum wages. The minimum wage for enterprises ranged from 2.4 million VND ($108) per month to 3.5 million VND ($157) per month, depending on the region. In August the National Wages Council agreed to a 7.3 percent increase in the minimum wage, to take effect on January 1, 2017, bringing the minimum wage range to 2.58 million VND ($116) to 3.76 million VND ($169) per month.

The law sets normal hours of work at eight hours per day, with a mandatory 24-hour break each week. Additional hours require overtime pay at one and one-half times the regular wage, two times the regular wage for working through the mandatory 24-hour rest period, and three times the regular wage for holidays and paid-leave days. The law limits overtime to 50 percent of normal working hours per day, 30 hours per month, and 200 hours per year, but it provides for an exception in special cases, with a maximum of 300 overtime hours worked annually, subject to stipulation by the government after consulting with the VGCL and employer representatives. The law also prescribes 12 to 16 days of annual leave, depending on the type of work.

In July the country's first law on occupational safety and health, which also extends legal protections and accident prevention efforts to the informal economy, came into force. The law regulates the work of providing for occupational safety and health, describes procedures for persons who are victims of labor accidents and occupational diseases, and delineates the responsibilities of organizations and individuals in the occupational safety and health fields. The law provides for the right of workers to remove themselves from situations that endanger health or safety without jeopardy to their employment. The law protects "labor subleasing" as a new pattern of employment and thus extends protection to part-time and domestic workers.

The Ministry of Labor is the principal labor authority, and it oversees the enforcement of the labor law, administers labor relations policy, and promotes job creation. The ministry is responsible for providing technical support to and overseeing 63 provincial departments of labor, invalids and social affairs, which belong to provincial people's committees. The Labor Inspections Department is composed of labor inspectorates in the ministry at the central level and labor departments at the provincial level. Labor inspectors are responsible for conducting inspections in accordance with the annual plans of the ministry or labor departments to oversee compliance with labor laws, including occupational safety and health laws, payment of social security dues, responding to complaints alleging labor law violations, and investigating occupational accidents. Labor legislation is enforced by inspectors authorized to use sanctions, including oral and written warnings, fines, withdrawal of operating licenses or registrations, closures of enterprises, and mandatory training. Inspectors can take immediate measures where they have reason to believe there is an imminent and serious danger to the health or safety of workers, including temporarily suspending operations, although such measures were rare. According to labor ministry officials, there were more than 500 labor inspectors nationwide, including both full- and part-time inspectors.

It was unclear how strictly the government enforced provisions for wages, hours, and benefits or occupational safety and health restrictions, including in the informal economy. Enforcement was irregular for many reasons, including low funding and a shortage of trained enforcement personnel. The VGCL asserted authorities did not always prosecute violations. The ministry acknowledged shortcomings in its labor inspection system and emphasized the number of labor inspectors countrywide was insufficient. The VGCL stated, and the ministry acknowledged, fines on firms for labor violations were too low to act as an effective deterrent against violations. Fines generally range from 1.065 million to 106.5 million VND ($48 to $4,800), depending on the offense.

There continued to be credible reports that factories exceeded legal overtime thresholds and did not meet legal requirements for rest days, including in a 2016 impact evaluation of the ILO's Better Work program. That report also found, however, that workers in participating garment-producing factories reported working 55 hours per week by the fifth year of their factory's participation, a reduction of four hours per week from the baseline. According to the report, 62.8 percent of participating garment-producing factories were noncompliant in at least one aspect of overtime wage payments. The report stated that the major factor behind the noncompliance was the use of incorrect and unlawful salary calculation formulas, which led to incorrect payment of overtime wages. The report also found that the payment of minimum wages was generally an area of high compliance across Better Work factories. Ten percent of Better Work factories were noncompliant on minimum wage payments for regular full-time workers, likely because of incorrect salary calculation forms.

Migrant workers, including internal economic migrants, were among the most vulnerable workers, and employers routinely subjected them to hazardous working conditions. Other workers who often worked in the informal economy included members of ethnic minority groups. According to the ILO, informal workers in the country typically had low and irregular incomes, endured long working hours, and lacked protection by labor market institutions. On-the-job injuries due to poor health and safety conditions and inadequate employee training remained a problem. In the first six months of the year, the government reported 3,674 occupational accidents with 3,777 victims, including 332 fatal incidents with 356 deaths. Serious cases included a stone mine accident in Thanh Hoa Province in January, where a gas leak killed eight workers. The Ministry of Labor estimated that 60 workers died every month in industrial accidents.